Creative Approaches to Teachii

Creative Approaches to Teaching Grammar is an easily accessible, practical guide full of ideas to support teachers in making the learning of grammar a natural part of developing their students as writers and as readers. Written for those teaching years 5, 6, 7 and 8, the authors' approach concentrates on the individual needs of students rather than of a year group as a whole.

Split into two main sections, the first section looks at creative ways of exploring grammar and includes more than forty ideas that can be implemented into the classroom. This section can be used as a quick resource or the whole sequence can be followed to ensure students are investigating, exploring and having fun with grammar.

The second section includes an extensive glossary of terms to develop a full understanding of grammar, which can be used to audit your own competences and highlight areas for further development.

Creative ideas explored include:

- being silly with grammar
- favourite words
- exploding sentences
- writing for real audiences
- new punctuation marks and emoticons
- sorting out confusing words
- broadening active vocabulary
- ten tips for spelling
- flexing your vocabulary brain
- redundancy in language.

Creative Approaches to Teaching Grammar is a truly practical guide that is a must read for anyone teaching grammar to years 5, 6, 7 and 8. With plenty of ideas to implement into the classroom it encourages students to take ownership of their own learning and progress.

Martin Illingworth is Senior Lecturer in English Education at Sheffield Hallam University, UK.

Nick Hall is the Director of Teach First East Midlands, UK.

NATE

The National Association for the Teaching of English (NATE), founded in 1963, is the professional body for all teachers of English from primary to Post-16. Through its regions, committees and conferences, the association draws on the work of classroom practitioners, advisers, consultants, teacher trainers, academics and researchers to promote dynamic and progressive approaches to the subject by means of debate, training and publications. NATE is a charity reliant on membership subscriptions. If you teach English in any capacity, please visit **www.nate.org.uk** and consider joining NATE, so the association can continue its work and give teachers of English and the subject a strong voice nationally.

This series of books co-published with NATE reflects the organisation's dedication to promoting standards of excellence in the teaching of English, from early years through to university level. Titles in this series promote innovative and original ideas that have practical classroom outcomes and support teachers' own professional development.

Books in the NATE series include both pupil and classroom resources and academic research aimed at English teachers, students on PGCE/ITT courses and NQTs.

Titles in this series include:

International Perspectives on Teaching English in a Globalised World
Andrew Goodwyn, Louann Reid and Cal Durrant

Teaching English Language 16–19
Martin Illingworth and Nick Hall

Unlocking Poetry (CD-ROM)
Trevor Millum and Chris Warren

Teaching English Literature 16–19
Carol Atherton, Andrew Green and Gary Snapper

Teaching Caribbean Poetry
Beverley Bryan and Morag Styles

Sharing not Staring, 2nd Edition
Trevor Millum and Chris Warren

Teaching Grammar Structure and Meaning
Marcello Giovanelli

Researching and Teaching Reading
Gabrielle Cliff Hodges

Introducing Teacher's Writing Groups
Jenifer Smith and Simon Wrigley

Creative Approaches to Teaching Grammar
Martin Illingworth and Nick Hall

Creative Approaches to Teaching Grammar

Developing your students as writers and readers

Martin Illingworth and Nick Hall

Routledge
Taylor & Francis Group
LONDON AND NEW YORK

NATE

First published 2016
by Routledge
2 Park Square, Milton Park, Abingdon, Oxon OX14 4RN

and by Routledge
711 Third Avenue, New York, NY 10017

Routledge is an imprint of the Taylor & Francis Group, an informa business

British Library Cataloguing in Publication Data
A catalogue record for this book is available from the British Library

Library of Congress Cataloging in Publication Data
Illingworth, Martin.
Creative approaches to teaching grammar : developing your students as writers and readers / Martin Illingworth and Nick Hall.
pages cm
1. English language—Grammar—Study and teaching. 2. English language—Composition and exercises—Study and teaching. I. Hall, Nick. II. Title.
LB1576.I38 2016
372.4—dc23
2015024487

ISBN: 978-1-138-81928-3 (hbk)
ISBN: 978-1-138-81929-0 (pbk)
ISBN: 978-1-315-74466-7 (ebk)

Typeset in Galliard
by FiSH Books Ltd, Enfield

Printed and bound by Ashford Colour Press Ltd., Gosport, Hampshire.

MIX
Paper from
responsible sources
FSC® C011748

This book is dedicated to all those called Illingworth, Ormsby-Ashworth, Ansell, Walters and Oakes that I get to call my family. Thank you.

Martin Illingworth

This book is dedicated to the people that made it possible for me to write it; my parents, Robert and Maureen Hall for their unfailing support, my colleagues over the years who have been open-minded enough to listen to my ideas, and the students with whom I have spent many happy, challenging and stimulating hours in English classrooms.

Nick Hall

Contents

Introduction   1
Teachers of Key Stage 2   3
Teachers of Key Stage 3   5
The problem with transition   7
Auditing your knowledge   9
Levels of understanding in testing   12
Relevance   14

Ideas for teaching grammar   17

1   Questioning   19
2   Sentences   21
3   Marginal commentaries   24
4   Collecting signs   26
5   Guiding the reader   29
6   The grammar of speech   31
7   Being silly with grammar   33
8   Your attitude towards grammar   35
9   Favourite words   37
10 Syntax   39
11 Dictionaries   41
12 Stop PEE-ing!   43
13 Significance and value   45
14 Exploding sentences   47
15 Grammar working wall   49
16 Finding your voices – auto/biography   51
17 Handwriting   53
18 Writing for real audiences   55
19 Chasing the dream   57
20 Telling stories   59
21 Twitter stories   61
22 Just because it is   65

23   New punctuation marks and emoticons   67
24   Grammar t-shirts   70
25   Sorting out confusing words   72
26   High-frequency language   73
27   Broadening active vocabulary   75
28   Re/drafting   77
29   Patterns and exceptions   80
30   Ten tips for spellings   82
31   Big, deep and wide questions   85
32   Making up new words   87
33   Difficult words/punctuation   89
34   Cut and paste fun   91
35   Dramatic readings   93
36   The grammar of photography   95
37   Innate competence   97
38   Playing with word class   100
39   Explicit modelling of writing   103
40   Ask the author   105
41   Flexing your vocabulary brain   107
42   Redundancy in language   109

Glossary   113

A glossary of terms   115

Index   137

Introduction

The teaching of grammar has always been a hotly debated part of the curriculum. There have been times when explicit understanding of how our language is constructed was not on the curriculum at all. The innate nature of grammar making was thought to support a curriculum that was more interested in personal expression. There have also been times, as now, when knowing the terminology is foregrounded. The current government documentation around the testing at the end of Key Stage 2 has a glossary of 59 technical terms. The testing requires explicit knowledge of this set of terms.

The intention of this book is to support teachers (you) in making the learning of grammar a natural part of developing your students as writers and as readers. We want our young people to have the best possible capability as communicators and inter-preters of language. The twenty-first century offers so many ways to communicate, so many ways to access the world, that our students need to be able to join in effectively if they are to flourish. Articulacy is the route towards empowering your students to be resourceful enough to grasp the opportunities that come their way. An appreciation of grammar supports this aim.

There are two broad sections to our book. First, we offer you some creative ways of exploring grammar. Students today are less likely than ever to sit quietly and be lectured at. Schooling is just an ever-smaller part of the ecosystem of learning. There are so many other places that students can access learning. In most of those other places they are also able to choose what they learn. It is our belief that your students will engage better with your lessons if they are seeking out new knowledge rather than receiving old knowledge. They will start to take ownership of their learning. Many of the ideas in the first section of the book offer that potential. These ideas are aimed at students in Years 5, 6, 7 and 8. Any of the ideas might be used for any of the years. You know that students will develop at different rates and that to some extent the whole idea of educating students in batches of year groups is an artificial construct. This section is organised in such a way that you can dip in by interest to single sections or you can follow the whole sequence through, which will hopefully allow you to get a sense of the thinking behind allowing students to investigate, explore and have fun.

Second, we have included a glossary of terms for your use in developing your own understanding of grammar. You could use it to audit your competences and areas of further development. You could dip into it as the need arises. We certainly do not intend for you to pass the glossary on to your students. Hopefully, this is a book of thinking. We would like you to think through the potential ways you can package the learning so that it is relevant to the lives that your students are living.

Too many children are going to tests in a state of alarm; some can't sleep for nights before, some are sick on the way to school. The high-stakes testing culture has created this anxiety and unhappiness. We hope that this book will help you see the potential of young people becoming linguists rather than test-takers.

Teachers of Key Stage 2

An understanding of standard written grammar is a functional part of the wider concern of developing the capabilities of writers and readers. When one word is put next to another, the meaning of each is altered. This is the basic function of grammar; constructing meaning through ordering vocabulary, sentences and whole texts. Evidently, there is much more to writing when trying to shape language to have an intended impact upon a reader. The grammatical structures are the foundation upon which meaning can be organised and developed.

Spelling, punctuation and grammar are back in the educational spotlight. High-stakes testing in Year 6, with implications for primary school league tables, has re-created an approach to teaching grammar in a de-contextualised, stand-alone manner. The pressures to achieve good marks in the test have meant that teachers have once again been left in the position of 'gaming the system'. The practical thing to do in this set of circumstances has been to teach grammar in discrete lessons so as to prepare for the testing that follows. The value of this systematic teaching is very much up for debate. Whilst educationalists are more interested in setting the teaching of grammar within the contexts in which it will be employed, the government want to test declarative knowledge in isolation.

The Year 6 SP&G test makes use of sentences that do not have any contextual back-ground. Students are asked to insert words, underline words, put in appropriate words and so on. This is a test that is easy to mark and is meant to have right or wrong answers; making the results 'reliable' against each other. Some feel that the test is more for the purpose of recording the achievements of the school than for developing the capabilities of the students to become confident creators and interpreters of texts.

Another important issue that has arisen from this recent interest in grammar teaching is that of teacher confidence. Uncertain linguistic knowledge has meant that teachers do not always feel confident enough to explain the terminology required effectively and in then demonstrating how linguistic devices can be employed in practice. A range of recent research suggests that, unsurprisingly

> students in intervention classes with teachers with higher knowledge benefitted more than those with teachers who had lower subject knowledge.

Without strong subject knowledge, teachers can end up making confusing and unhelpful remarks about the use of grammatical structures and devices.

There is clear sense in teaching grammar explicitly and doing so in the context of developing students' abilities to write and to read. Whilst the testing of eleven-year olds on a potential pool of 59 terms of grammar seems a somewhat thin aim in terms of developing writers and readers in the twenty-first century, it does mean that students have a heightened awareness of the structures of language. The key issue here is that this declarative knowledge must lead to procedural knowledge; an actual ability to transfer this isolated set of rules to the practical world of creating and interpreting texts.

Teachers of Key Stage 3

When your new Year 7 class arrives with their brand-new pencil cases, slightly too big uniforms and nerves about their new environment you may well have made assumptions about them. These may be based on your previous experience of new Year 7s, what you have heard anecdotally, the 'data' that you have seen on them or your thoughts and understanding of their experience of school life up to the age of eleven.

Those assumptions will say an awful lot about you too, and it is those thoughts that this passage is intended to address.

In Year 6 your new pupils will have been studying hard for their SATS to ensure that they achieve the level that best represents, to you, how capable they are at English. An important and new element of this testing is the focus on spelling, punctuation and grammar. They may have been through a hot-house of exam preparation where everything focused on the test. They may have felt the pressure that their teacher was feeling. It may be the case that they were taught to love language, to revel in reading and to discuss their understanding of texts freely with their peers in an intellectually challenging environment. Some pupils may hate school, some may love it. Some may have supportive and encouraging parents, others less so. The one thing that can be assumed with certainty is that you will be teaching a diverse group of young people, all of whom bring their own experiences and assumptions too.

All great teaching is built on great relationships. The initial stages of those relationships are as critical as the constant maintenance and updating of them that continues throughout the school year. The work that is required here of a Year 7 teacher should never be underestimated. This is the learning that helps us to navigate through and beyond those early assumptions. You may have them confirmed, challenged, reinforced and dismantled as the year goes on. Your teaching will certainly be moving those pupils on through the next stage of their development as readers, writers and talkers. The time and energy that you will put in to these young people is not to be underestimated, nor is the task ahead of you. As they move through Years 7 and 8 – the only years that remain as truly Key Stage 3 – your classes are on the leg of their learning journey from primary school pupils to GCSE students. It is crucial that this leg is designed to build on the talents and understanding that have been developed by your peers in the primary sector.

This book is designed to support you as you prepare to plan and teach English to children at this stage of their development. Our intention in writing it is to contribute to a developing understanding of how best to continue the learning that has already happened, especially in the specialist areas of spelling, punctuation and grammar. It is a map, with successful routes already highlighted, alongside many other possible routes that you can determine to best meet the needs of the young people for whom you are accountable.

The problem with transition

At the age of 11 most school pupils make the move from their primary school, where they have learned to read and write, built friendships and developed as thinkers, to their secondary school. This is where the remainder of their formal education will be completed. Of course, this simple story is rather more complicated for many young people whose parents migrate from one location to another or who choose to move establishments and attend schools or colleges that don't quite fit the standard pattern of the 5–11 and 11–18 system.

Moving from one establishment to another is shrouded in the metaphor of transition. A quick look at a thesaurus and the inferences of transition are laid bare: change, metamorphosis, mutation, conversion and modification are alternatives for the process that so many children encounter as one phase of schooling ends and another begins. Children do not metamorphose during the summer break separating Year 6 and Year 7. The institution they attend changes, they don't.

Maintaining the metaphor of transition endangers the likelihood of educational continuity. Moving to another school should represent a continuation of the work that all young people and their teachers have undertaken. It should be a moment where children experience and can articulate the ways that their teachers have ensured continuity. The risk of maintaining the metaphor of transition is that the community of teachers continue to condemn children to unnecessary pedagogical readjustments. Our profession needs to undergo a transition, not hundreds of thousands of children every summer.

Throw in the complexity and uncertainty that characterises a sector in a state of constant change and the requirement for teachers and schools at a local level to share approaches becomes ever stronger. Long, long gone are the days that a 'transition unit' could be taught for a few weeks at the end of Year 6 and completed in the few weeks at the start of Year 7. Structural reforms since 2010 make the landscape increasingly interesting for those of us concerned with educational continuity between Years 6 and 7. This book makes a contribution, albeit modest, to that cause.

Most Year 6 teachers will say farewell to their class in July knowing that the children will be moving to several different schools to continue their education. Most Year 7 teachers will welcome their classes in September knowing that they arrive having been taught at any number of different primary schools. For those children who attend all-through schools this challenge will be significantly reduced, though not to the extent that the issue is removed. By following the ideas in this book, teachers working with children on either side of what has previously been called 'transition', can ensure the lurch from one institution to another can become more of a side-step.

The book is intended to enable the students in your classes to become proficient users and explainers of grammar. To demonstrate those skills, students need to have a working understanding of all of the terms and concepts that make up language. Acquiring a lifelong ability as a linguist starts here and fortunately for everyone, doing so will ensure that the kids do really well in their tests, too.

Auditing your knowledge

Here is an audit of the sorts of learning that the students will need to consider for the Key Stage 2 SP&G testing that Year 6 students undergo in the May before they head off to high school, or when they are about to move in to the top two years of middle school. The categories are taken from the English SP&G test framework published by the Standards and Testing Agency. They have made use of the Key Stage 2 programme of study in identifying what areas of the curriculum are being addressed.

We have adapted the documentation so that you can think through those areas that you are confident in and also so you can consider areas that you will need to investigate if you are to be accurate and helpful in the classroom. A firm understanding will support you in creating valuable lesson ideas.

Whilst reading through this sequence, you might like to make a 'shopping list' of the things that you are not sure about so that you can brush up with further study.

Word classes and the grammatical functions of words

You need to be able to get your students to distinguish between the different types, or classes, of words. This would include nouns, pronouns, verbs, adverbs, adjectives, prepositions, conjunctions and articles.

Your students should have experience of investigating the features of different types of sentence. This would include recognising and being able to produce statements, questions and commands.

The grammar of complex sentences needs to be explored. Students should have the chance to demonstrate that they are able to recognise types of clauses, phrases and the use of connectives.

Standard forms of English

Students will be expected to have an understanding of how written standard English varies in degrees of its formality and that the domains of formality have become fewer.

You need to be able to discuss some of the differences between standard English and non-standard English usage.

Students need to be familiar with tense agreement, subject-verb agreement, double negatives, the use of 'I' and 'me' and contractions.

Vocabulary and strategies around language usage

Will you be able to support your students in broadening their active vocabulary and in helping them to use that vocabulary in inventive ways?

Your students need to be encouraged to proofread their own writing, checking their drafts for spelling and punctuation errors, omissions and repetitions.

Your students need to investigate vocabulary. They need to have strategies to find out the meanings of words. They should have the opportunity to examine words in their contexts, exploring the employment of words by writers.

In particular, the Key Stage 2 programme of study requires students to have an explicit and a working knowledge of concision and precision in vocabulary, synonyms, antonyms, word groups/families, prefixes, suffixes and the making of singular and plural forms. Again, think through where you are clear and where you will need to do some research.

Punctuation

Your students need to develop approaches and strategies so that they are able to make appropriate use of punctuation marks in their writing.

This would include being able to employ full stops, question and exclamation marks, commas, inverted commas, and apostrophes to mark possession and omission.

Capital letters
Full stops
Question marks
Exclamation marks
Commas in lists
Commas to mark phrases or clauses
Inverted commas
Apostrophes
Brackets
Ellipsis
Colons

Spelling strategies

The Key Stage 2 strategy suggests a number of ways of approaching the active remembering of spellings. These include the following:

• sounding out phonemes to construct a word from its constituent sounds;

- analysing words into syllables and other known words;
- developing and then applying growing knowledge of spelling conventions and patterns;
- using knowledge of common letter strings, visual patterns and analogies;
- supporting your students to check their own spelling;
- considering the spelling of words with inflectional endings.

You need to feel confident across each of these areas. Your confidence is not just about being able to fend off difficult questions from students. It is about informing the process of making valuable lesson ideas.

Levels of understanding in testing

The documentation around the SP&G tests offers a description of the sorts of questioning that will be in the test papers. Known as the 'cognitive level' it classifies the 'difficultness' of question types within a six-point taxonomy, derived from Bloom's cognitive domain. Knowing how the questions will be phrased and the thinking that has gone on to answer successfully is an important insight into preparing your own work in the classroom.

Here is an explanation of the cognitive levels.

1. The most straightforward of the levels is **Knowledge**. This is the checking of declarative knowledge. Are your students able to identify terminology and functions of language? Examples might include:

   - What is the name of the punctuation mark in the sentence below?
   - Put a circle round the adjective in the following sentence.
   - Which word, from the list below, correctly completes the sentence?

2. The next level checks **Comprehension.** Is there an understanding of the workings of words and grammatical structures? Examples might include:

   - Circle the word that is being used to describe …
   - Tick the word that means …

3. Do your students have procedural knowledge? By this, we mean, can they apply their knowledge past identifying features. This level is called **Application**. Examples might include:

   - Complete the sentence below with an adjective that makes sense.

   In the example above, your student needs to know what an adjective is, what its function is and then has to be able to apply that understanding to a new situation.

   - Write a complex sentence using the connective 'because'.

Similarly, your student needs to know what the function of a connective is and then needs to apply this knowledge to a new sentence.

- Which sentence uses inverted commas correctly?

4. Are your students able to analyse language? This is exactly the sort of approach that many of the ideas in this book promote. It is that sifting and sorting of autonomous investigative learning that prepares students for this higher order skill set. This level is called **Analysis**. Examples would include:

- Categorise these into adverbs of time, place and manner.
- Why is a colon being used in the sentence below?

5. The next level involves the process of **Synthesis**. Making use of understanding across the range of their grammatical understanding, can your students bring their understanding to bear on a problem? Examples might include:

- How could the clarity of the following sentence be improved? Re-write it, making changes to punctuation and wording to make it clearer.

6. Finally, we have the level of **Evaluation**. Students are encouraged to think creatively in approaching language use. For example:

- What would be the effect of replacing the commas in this sentence with dashes?

These are the 'levels' at which questioning is going to take place in the tests. Are you able to build into your lesson sequences opportunities to think in these different ways and to demonstrate understanding in these different ways?

Relevance

When your child is young you show them how a cup of tea is made. Why do you do that? At first, it is to do with safety. The kettle is hot, you don't want them to get burnt. They need an awareness of this aspect of making tea. Then, as they grow older they may acquire a taste for tea and want to drink it. It would be useful to be able to make their own – even make a cup or two for you! They can then develop their understanding that there is a range of types of tea available. They can develop their tastes. This is deemed fairly essential knowledge and we all find out about how to make a cup of tea in the normal run of things. Less essential to this operation is an understanding of how kettles are made or how they work. This is more specialist knowledge that we would only really pursue if we were to move into a related field of employment. Most people happily operate a kettle without this specialist knowledge. Again, in the making of the tea there is no test of how to operate the kettle or how it was constructed.

The example above is of learning that a parent deems necessary for safety and convenience. Life skills that everyone needs. Interestingly, there is no test for this. Your child receives guidance, is supervised and then allowed to develop their abilities in tea making. No test of either essential or specialist knowledge.

Imagine – if you will – an education system without testing. Children are offered experiences of essential, and sometimes specialist, knowledge but no one is tested. Difficult to imagine in our present schooling set up. It strikes us that the teaching of grammar to nine- to thirteen-year olds needs to be restricted to those elements that are 'essential' for them to know, for their well-being, safety and understanding.

In our testless schooling system, what do you think essential to know? What knowledge and understanding will support their development as communicators? Specialist knowledge can come later and just for those who will work with language, and who need a language with which to describe language. After all, we don't all need to know how to make a microwave oven to use one. Here we have the acid test for the grammar curriculum. If there was no test what would you keep in? Your answer to this question is the route to articulacy.

Here is a term that teachers are asked to teach to their Year 6 students. If there were no test would you deem this essential or specialist knowledge?

Schwa

The name of a vowel sound that is found only in unstressed positions in English. It is the most common vowel sound in English. It is written as /ə/ in the International Phonetic Alphabet. In the English writing system, it can be written in many different ways.

/əlɒŋ/ [along]
/bʌtə/ [butter]
/dɒktə/ [doctor]

An activity that might help you to plan might be to look through the glossary that we offer you here and select the areas of grammar that you think 'essential'. Perhaps you can build a curriculum around your list. Prioritising in this way can help you develop the sense of relevance that grammar study can have.

Ideas for teaching grammar

Questioning

Working to the assumption that a section on open and closed questions would be somewhat redundant here, let's focus on how you and your students can ask and analyse questions to develop knowledge of grammar alongside the topic being studied.

Imagine that you are working on the topic of 'chocolate' for this half term. The topic could take you through the history of chocolate production and the geography of cocoa cultivation, through the marketing of chocolate products and the health effects of chocolate consumption. I'm fairly sure that it will be possible to work in some tasting either during the lessons or if not, during their preparation. Having undertaken the introduction to the topic you will inevitably ask the class some questions. Alongside your consideration of asking challenging, open questions, you could consider the impact that modal verbs will have on the discussion.

The modal verbs are: *can, could, may, might, shall, should, will, would.* As a literacy objective throughout the unit of work, a clear focus on modal verbs will unlock thinking about both the topic and the methods of study. Having shared or co-created your objectives, you can pose a series of questions that use modal verbs to enable the students to consider their learning.

How **can** we understand the effects chocolate has on our bodies?
Can we use drama to learn about this topic?

We **may** use maps, how **might** they help our learning?

When **shall** we use internet research?
Shall we bring any experts in to the lessons?

Will we be able to find out who first ate chocolate?
What **would** be the best assessment method at the end of the unit?

This deliberate construction of questions employing modal verbs instigates a sense of enquiry in the students and a sense of ownership over their learning.

This focus on a sense of possibility can be enhanced when, later in the half term, the students are undertaking independent group work and you provide them with stimulus questions. Enabling your students to focus on how they operate as group, rather than simply the physical outcomes of their work, can be transformative. If the physical outcome is something along the lines of presenting an understanding of the journey a cocoa bean makes from plant to shop, the stimulus you pose could again draw on the wonders of modal verbs.

> **Could** you ascribe roles that let everyone play to their strengths?
> **Might** you design your own measures of success?
> **Should** you look for any help or support from outside of your group?
> **Would** it be helpful to see how other groups are working?

Having embedded modality as a feature of the unit of work, it will be time for the students to start to experiment with the creation of questions that feature modal verbs. This will create the opportunity for them to take the work far beyond the normal limits of discovering historical, geographical, physiological and marketable details of chocolate production. Each group should define the scope of their projects by setting themselves research questions using modal constructions. They should also pose questions to which they don't know the answer.

> **Could** we persuade the marketing team at *X manufacturer* to use our ideas to sell their products?
> How **might** history help us to understand why chocolate is important to today's consumers?
> **Should** we care about where our chocolate comes from?
> **Would** eating more or less chocolate make us healthier?

These big questions demand creative thinking and creative approaches to evaluating the knowledge that is acquired through research. The first question to be asked following the creation of a big research question is 'What do we need to know to answer the question?' Answering this question determines a methodology and from there roles can be assigned, learning can continue with a clear focus and modal verbs have underpinned some challenging investigative learning.

Sentences

A qualified mathematician may offer a more sophisticated analysis than this, though for our purposes it's pretty much true to claim that there is an infinite number of sentences that can be crafted. It is probably the case that the previous sentence is unique – a collection of words that have never been put together in that order. Fortunately for budding writers in your class there are ways to classify sentences. An active knowledge of these classifications will enable them to consciously manipulate grammatical structures to create deliberate effects.

This section will cover the three types of sentence we have in English alongside active and passive forms. A helpful critical standpoint is to consider all sentences equal. Complex sentences are not intrinsically better than simple sentences; active constructions are not better than passive. With this perspective a writer can be free to choose the best construction for the purposes of their writing rather than feeling constrained by the need to demonstrate a range of sentences to satisfy a mark scheme. Freedom from constraint coupled with grammatical understanding will result in quality writing.

A quick recap:

- Simple sentences contain a single statement, as in *Helen's students thought that she was a bit crazy.*
- Compound sentences contain more than one single statement, as in *English is Tom's favourite subject because he gets to write stories.*
- Complex sentences contain a main clause coupled with one or more subordinate clauses, as in *To fulfil her ambition to study Maths at university, Rubinder worked really hard at school,* or *The gardens are beautiful when the sun shines.*

Writers need to choose the most appropriate construction to create the effect intended. Let's look to a master of the craft, Philip Pullman. In his retelling of *Snow White*, Pullman opens the tale with a richly detailed complex sentence.[1]

One winter's day, when the snowflakes were falling like feathers, a queen sat sewing at her window, which had a frame of the blackest ebony.

In the first subordinate clause the reader is given detail about time, in the second the weather and it is only in the third and main clause that we meet the subject of the sentence, 'a queen' with complementary detail about what she is doing and in the final subordinate clause more detail. This is expert storytelling through grammatical choices. The reader is rapidly brought in to the text-world through clauses that quickly zoom in from the broad to the precise and finally zooming back out to frame the queen in ebony. If you or your students rewrote this introduction as four simple sentences the pace and relationships between the elements would be lost. Later in the tale when the mirror tells the queen that Snow White is the fairest of all and she summons a huntsman to kill Snow White, Pullman writes,

The huntsman did as she ordered.

Here, the simple sentence is perfect. It captures the drama and grimness of the situation Snow White faces. This effect is redoubled as simple sentences are rare things in Pullman's version of this tale. He seems to be reserving them for very special occasions. Later, following the huntsman's failure to carry out his orders, the queen herself tries to kill Snow White. The dwarves return to find her nearly suffocated and release her.

Little by little she came back to life and told them what had happened.

This straightforward narrative sentence works as a compound construction; the reader is given sequential pieces of detail, the story moves on apace and the reader is led through the narrative.

With these examples, you can share this discussion with your students. Read them the story in full and tease out the way that Pullman manipulates grammatical constructions to create particular effects. Armed with increasing expertise, it'll be time for the students to explore how they can develop the same skill.

For the purposes of this activity, it will be helpful for all children to be writing about the same, tightly limited, topic. Fairy stories provide good source material, as would a non-fiction piece such as a newspaper article. As ever, the ideas can be applied to any relevant topic you're working on. You need to present a simplified structure for your young writers to build up in to narrative. An example might look like:

CHILD ➡ WOODS ➡ FEAR ➡ ENCOUNTER ➡ ESCAPE

It is important not to do any writing. At least, it's important that children don't start writing as individuals and that no one commits words to the page or screen until there's been some talk and play. Depending on your students' needs, either:

- Use the words in Table 2.1 to physically create some sentences. Give the words and punctuation marks out, one to each child, and the kids can put themselves in order to create sentences. Start with simple sentences, for instance six students stand in a row holding the words *she walked along the path*. If they stay in place, other students can join in. Two join the front of the sentence to create *trembling, she walked along the path*. You now have material for discussion and will be building an understanding that we need to play around with word order and sentence structure if we are to be in control of the texts we create. You could instruct *trembling* to stand after *the* or to move with the comma to stand after *path*. The discussions you lead will result in more playful writers.

OR

• In pairs and using the same bank of words but this time recreated smaller, guide the pupils to create some sentences in the same way as the activity above, only at their desks. You can stop the work regularly and ask students to explain what they are currently thinking, and how they are succeeding in creating new sentences by messing around with word order, conjunctions and subordinate clauses.

You can, of course, use both ideas alongside one another. The most important development of either activity is the concept of rehearsal. Stopping to talk, think, play with word order before committing a sentence to the page is absolutely vital. You should be expecting to see children stopping to look at the ceiling, out of the window or close their eyes for a moment to think. Encourage it. Slowing down the writing process at the developmental stage means that your students will become highly competent and the skills they develop will become more immediate with practice. This is good old-fashioned quality over quantity.

Table 2.1 Making sentences

trembling	she	walked	along
flowers	he	ran	through
red	path	laughed	between
green	woods	the	a
white	trees	the	a
black	was	the	a
there	because	wild	light
rose	when	good	dark
snow	sun	rabbit	for
white	if	that	were
;	;	?	!
.	.	.	.
,	,	,	,

Note

1   Philip Pullman, *Grimm Tales: For Young and Old*, Penguin Classics, London (2013).

Marginal commentaries

Gauging the current capacities of a child in terms of their language development can be difficult. Devising activities to make explicit where they are 'up to' will mean that you can design appropriate steps forward. When students come to you they will have all sorts of capabilities and different ways of perceiving what they can and can't do. You need to get a handle on this prior learning quickly so that you are not faced with a sea of faces telling you that, 'We did this last year, miss'. Tuning in to current ability and experience will allow you to make use of what they are able to do and think about.

Here is an idea that allows your students to articulate their understanding of how they write. Your students have produced a piece of writing for you. You can apply this activity to whatever type of writing it is that you have been looking at. Get the students to type the text on this occasion. Once they have finished ask them to use the Comment feature to discuss the decisions that they have made in writing the piece.

This activity can be as prescriptive or free as you want. It is interesting to see what students come up with if you just ask them to comment on how they have pieced together the writing. From their choices of what to tell you, you will be able to gauge what they think is involved in constructing writing and also their level of confidence in discussing this issue. Will they stick to talking about spellings and making interesting sentences or will there be an awareness of audience and the potential of different ways of approaching their readership?

You could narrow the focus, asking students to think through a particular aspect of their writing. Perhaps they could tell you how they have decided to appeal to their audience. What are the features of their writing that help make that approach? Are there particular sentences that carry the message? How have they built the argument through the piece?

Hopefully, you can see the merits of this activity. Your students will demonstrate their abilities in assessing for themselves how writing works. From this starting point you will be able to pursue aspects of writing that they have yet to think through.

We think that your students will enjoy this kind of reflection on their own writing. It hands the mantle of expert over to them. Rather than it being you who makes the judgements about what they have written, they are able to explain to you what has happened. A refreshing change from having their work 'marked' all the time!

The use of technology is also motivating for your students. You know that the endless sheets they are given to evaluate their work have lost their appeal. There seems to us a certain detachment for students in many of the ways that they are offered to reflect on their progress. Saying whether you have reached 'Red', 'Amber' or 'Green' from statements on the whiteboard seems a little abstract. This more practical application of thinking through their writing, with that writing in front of them, will seem much more useful to students than just saying whether they have met a learning objective.

Collecting signs

It is important that your students can see the point of what they are doing, past the four walls of the classroom. This includes making learning about more than passing the test that is coming up. Schools are abstract places: lessons happen for a set amount of time and then, regardless of how finished an activity is, a bell rings and the students are asked to think about something else, to engage in another topic on another subject. You need to find ways of showing your students that the world past the door of your classroom needs the lessons learnt within it. Your students will always be, and mostly sub-consciously, looking for what matters, and, of course, what does not. You want your grammar sessions to be in the matters section of their brain's filing cabinet.

Asking your students to collect signs is one way that you can achieve this. The world is full of signage and a good deal of it is funny!

The very act of sending your students off to look for a good sign to bring in to show the class immediately alerts your students to the linguistic world around them. In pursuing this activity they are actively examining the language structures around them, in the natural contexts in which they can be found and, importantly, your students are searching for the purposes of the signs. In seeking out signs that don't work or that appear funny, they are considering the effectiveness of the signs. Your students will be actively engaged in searching the real world for audiences, purposes and contexts. That is what 'English' is all about. The act of looking is the real success of this activity.

We promise you that when you set this as a homework it will be popular. This is one occasion when you are not asking students to write. That will prove popular in itself.

The context in which you are working is one in which 85 per cent of school children never use paper and pen except for working in school or in doing school homework. Indeed, the examples of funny signs will keep on coming long after the homework is set. Why don't you have a 'Whoops!' board with photographs of the funny signs? That makes it explicit that the activity is ongoing. Students will want to contribute their photos. Students will love being in a position of power for a change. The signs have got it wrong and the student knows it. It is nice for the student to be correcting the adult world.

How good is the sign in Figure 4.1? The adult world of the exam, telling children what is what and messing up on the sign outside the exam. Brilliant. This is the sort of thing that students will revel in finding. In my experience, a healthy competition can be sparked to find more and more, and to find the 'best' sign.

Figure 4.1

As well as a 'Whoops!' board you could have a 'Clever Signs' board. Obviously, signs have a visual element and there is a good deal of interplay between the words and the images. Your students could investigate images like Figure 4.2, considering the link between the words and the presentation of the words. In this case, there is only one word in the image. The rest of the picture adds meaning to the word. Could your students think about the relationship between the words and the images? Are the images a kind of grammar? Do they support the word giving it meaning? That is all 'grammar' is at root; organising the words.

Figure 4.2

Source: www.cadencearts.com/music/el_vez.jpg

Elvez is the Mexican Elvis. Opportunities for Elvis Presley to enliven the topic of grammar are opening up before our very eyes! Even the grammar correct on my laptop wants it to be Elvis. This image makes use of the colours of the Mexican flag and the style and imagery of the 1960s comeback Elvis. Discussing images makes your students think about what they are seeing. In the process they will be thinking about how words work; the function of the word. That is where meaning resides. Words have no meaning past their functions. As a group of language speakers we collectively decide what functions a word will have. A word in isolation needs context. The images here provide that support. Grammar in writing is all about supporting the function/meaning of the words.

Signs can help your students to think about the nature of language. The fact they are finding the signs helps to make the activity feel more 'real'. The students take ownership of the learning. The motivated always outperform the unmotivated – at all levels of notional ability. A genuine understanding of the way words are organised, or in some cases have failed to be organised effectively, is part of a critical mass of understanding that a student needs to piece together the various aspects of grammatical knowledge.

Guiding the reader

Schools are rich sources for stories. Playgrounds, corridors, staffrooms and classrooms all thrive on the stories that are shared in them. It's how relationships are sustained and is often the means of exploring content in lessons. The stories that feature in lessons as things to be written and studied are a part of the rich narrative culture of schools. That narrative culture is central to learning; it's important that links are made between every-day life and classroom narratives for it allows explicit points of learning to take place whilst building on familiar skills.

This section is about time, place and detail. It builds on students' ability to relay stories and gives some practical tips on how to integrate some key grammatical tech-niques. Ultimately the section is about helping students to find the balance between brevity and detail. These are important choices for a writer to be able to make for the ability to guide the reader depends upon a writer being in control of their craft.

Stories need characters, settings and events. There also needs to be relationships between these features and it is relative clauses that define these relationships. Relative clauses are subordinate clauses formed by using a relative pronoun, adjective or adverb, such as *who, whom, which, whose, that, when* and *where*. Taking a list of words that are required to form relative clauses is a good starting point. From there, a very simple narrative can be formed. To get used to the technique ask your students to recount a simple tale, such as their journey to school, using only simple sentences.

> A girl walked to school. [*Who*] She went past the pet shop. [*Where*] She started day-dreaming. [*What*] She did this every morning. [*When*] She arrived at school. [*Where*]

Those five sentences make for an entirely functional narrative. It only gives the reader the slightest insight in to the character, setting and events. It doesn't read very well either; it is stylistically unsatisfying and grammatically unsophisticated. Introducing the class to the effect of relative clauses will enable the students to create complex sentences, which will mean they can build upon the simplest of ideas to create engag-ing writing.

A girl *who dreamed of owning a kitten* walked to school. She went past the pet shop *which often had a 'Kittens for sale' sign in the window*. She started day-dreaming about the day *when a purring cat would sleep at her feet every night*. She did this every morning. She arrived at school *where friends and lessons distracted her from kitten-dreams*.

Now there is a story. Our protagonist has an identity, the setting has some detail to be pictured and there is a relationship between the sequenced events. Adding more details such as calling the girl *Amanda* or *Roisin* or *Angel*, naming the pet shop, the street, the school or the kitten would all add details that stimulate the reader's willingness to engage.

Getting the right level of detail in to a narrative is another crucial element of the craft of guiding readers. The old adage of *show don't tell* will always be true and teaching young writers how to achieve this is time well spent. Showing the reader how a character feels about a spider wandering down a wall, 'Andrew ran out the room' will always be more effective than telling the reader how 'Andrew is scared of spiders.' Even describing it as *wandering*, rather than the default *crawling*, shows the reader far more about an attitude to spiders than they could ever be told.

Showing rather than telling can be a useful concept for teaching the skill of offering the reader a level of detail that tells them what is happening in the story whilst leaving space for their imagination to do its work. It also helps with the avoidance of strings of adjectives. 'The big, brown, muscly snarling dog' seems far less effective than 'All Amy could focus on was the dog's teeth.' These are very different sentences, and the point that is being made is that students need to be able to manipulate these choices for themselves.

The grammar of speech

Writing assumes a privileged position when it comes to the valuing of speech and writing. Writing is the winner! This is because we have the innate ability to speak whilst we have to be taught the art of writing.

Writing is serious – there are structural rules to be followed, spellings to know and all kinds of ways to make mistakes and appear foolish. Writing is high stakes. It is an abstract skill – one that has to be learned, like riding a bike.

We perhaps take speech for granted because it comes so easily. By the time we are three, we are fully competent in expressing ourselves. No problem. Plus, 'speech doesn't have rules' your students might say!

Pose a question. What is the grammar of speech? After all, you don't need capital letters or paragraphs or full stops or any of the other ways of organising written language. So how exactly is it that we organise the words that we say?

Whilst it may not be obvious to your students, evidently speech has a system of grammatical structures. We speak in what are called utterances. The basic unit of a conversation in organising these utterances is a turn. All sorts of implicit rules apply to how conversations are conducted. Ask your students to think about how you indicate that you want to have a turn when someone else is speaking. Ask your students to consider what happens to the voice when you are coming to the end of your turn and you are indicating that you are going to let someone else have a go. What happens with the voice when someone chooses to interrupt?

Getting your students to make a transcript is a good way for them to think about the grammar of speech. Ask them to collect a recording of a person speaking. Here is an example.

> So his wife you know her she works at the coop on the deli counter anyway she has a brother and he turned up the other day at the gym big bloke he is but it turns out that he knows Sharon funny old world ain't it who'd a thought that he knows our Sharon he certainly didn't meet her in the gym she's never been near a gym she likes to ride her bike and does a bit of running but she's funny about gyms

How do you go about organising this stretch of speech to indicate the way that it was said? Your students need to devise a set of punctuation marks that indicate where the person put pauses in, the length of those pauses and where there was emphasis on a word. The pauses could be indicated with a set of brackets. In the brackets, your students could indicate lengthier pauses with the number of seconds between utterances. For example:

So his wife (3) you know her (1) she works at (2) the coop …

Either underlining or emboldening could function to show emphasis on a particular word or phrase.

who'd a thought that he knows **our Sharon** (3) he certainly didn't meet her in the gym **she's never been near a gym**

This kind of investigative approach to discovering the structures of speech will broaden the students' outlook on the idea of structures. It will, hopefully, make the structures of writing appear less authoritative and more like one of many approaches to organising language. Making comparison between the punctuation of writing with the punctuation of speech will allow your students to sift through the purposes of punctuation marks. They will be thinking through how we organise language. As with all of the investigative approaches offered here, the students' awareness of language more generally should develop.

Being silly with grammar

It might help the way students feel about grammar if we can have some fun, making use of our imaginations. Let's start with this: If you were leaving earth and moving to another planet, which punctuation mark would you take with you?

The question is silly but then kids love to be silly sometimes. However, in addressing the question the student has to think through which of the punctuation marks they think most useful. This kind of lateral, or abstract, thinking can broaden the concept that a student has of grammar.

Which of the punctuation marks would make the best rock star? Perhaps we could have a whole band! Which punctuation mark is the most fashionable? The most important? The most likely to get an OBE for services to the Queen?

Think of the endless ways that you as teacher could pack this idea up. Think of the endless ways that students could respond both verbally and in writing. Do you think that your students would be happy to use their imaginations in this way? We suspect that the answer is yes and that they would enjoy the abstract nature of your investigation into the make-up of grammar.

How about some news reporting? Interview Mr/Mrs/Ms Sentence to find out what job he/she does. What would be the problems caused if paragraphs went on strike?

And on and on we go!

Which is the punctuation mark that drives you crazy? Which verbs would be best in the army? Which punctuation mark would not be invited to your party? Which punctuation mark can you trust with your life?

These questions and ideas could make fabulous starters to get your students in the right frame of mind as they come into 'literacy' lessons and 'English' lessons. If they know there will be a fun approach they will soon get the idea and join in. We have given you ten ideas here but we are sure that you can think of hundreds more. We are sure that your students, once they have caught on, will be able to come up with their own imaginative challenges.

Too often it can be easy to overlook the power of a bit of fun. Teachers are under pressure to deliver 'results' and we can be very straightforward in getting straight to the learning objective by the shortest route. Such approaches can lack subtlety and lack the drive that an engaged imagination can bring to learning. Sometimes we as teachers need to believe/understand that a creative and expressive approach to developing linguistic interest in a student will have a huge impact upon their capacity to pass the inevitable testing.

Give it a try. It might be a novel approach but it is not a novelty. Making use of the imagination and the power of the abstract will make a difference.

Your attitude towards grammar

The way that you feel about the rather touchy subject of grammar might well be a starting point for you to reflect upon. Your disposition to being 'correct' is undoubtedly going to be passed on to your students. Your influence in this area is going to be undeniable; you are, after all, the teacher! That makes you the arbiter of 'rightness' in the eyes of your students.

A prescriptivist sensibility

Are you likely to value written standard grammar over spoken grammar? Will your outlook suggest that there are right and wrong ways to do things and that the rules of grammar are fixed and unmoveable? If the answer to that last question is yes, then that is your starting point. Whilst, on another day, we might take issue with your starting point, we/you need to acknowledge it and understand that your influence will be felt. It will set the parameters of how your students will see the overall place of grammatical structures in writing. You would look to address, in your classroom, areas of language production that students struggle to conform to the rules. An example here would be the apostrophe – a punctuation mark under wider threat in the world at large. You look to make plain the rules and then look for consistent application. A sense of a fixed set of rules that need to be followed is helpful in that it is consistent – until, of course, you get to the many irregular structures that English has developed.

A descriptivist approach

Are you more likely to see the range of ways that language users choose to organise their communication? With this attitude you will acknowledge that language is likely to change and that each generation of users adapts the language to make it easier to articulate. Both words and grammatical structures survive in a language only if they serve a purpose. You might suggest that the reason that the application of the apostrophe is struggling is because the apostrophe doesn't have any genuine function. You could take away the apostrophe and no sense of loss of communication would be felt. For example, 'wasnt' communicates no better than 'wasn't'. The reason that users are increasingly failing to use this punctuation mark is not to do with 'slovenly' attitudes to language. The language is just moving on.

A word of caution here: your students do need to pass their tests and as such they do need to know the standard forms of the written language at the time of the test to support passing it.

A balanced approach?

Can you see some middle ground? An awareness that language is not an entirely fixed system but that a standard will exist at any one time that users need to be able to access. This balance will help your students recognise how language works. As you are 'making' linguists this balance is important. It is also important to have discussions about how people see language. You and your students can spend time looking at the things that people say and at the ways that people feel about language. The internet, and media more broadly, is rife with examples of people and organisations quite prepared to say what they think about how people speak and write.

Here is one example: on 28 September 2010, the BBC reported that the actress Emma Thompson had 'spoken out' against the use of what she called 'sloppy language'.[1] It would be interesting to find out what your students think she might mean by that term. The article goes on to detail a visit that Emma Thompson made to her old school. Whilst at the school she told current students not to make use of 'slang words' such as 'likes' and 'innit'. She went on to tell them that those kinds of words '[make] you sound stupid and you're not stupid.' She went on to argue that, 'There is the necessity to have two languages – one that you use with your mates and the other that you need in any official capacity.' Perhaps your students would agree and could give examples of when they need to switch between these 'two languages'.

In discussing attitudes such as that expressed by Emma Thompson, you are able to get your students to think through what they think rather than just following what you might appear to think.

Note

1   You can find the article at www.bbc.co.uk/news/uk-11420737

Favourite words

It's hard not to have favourite words. They are often very personal. Words attached to experiences such as *birthdays, seaside* or *family*. Or words attached to people such as *grandson, partner* or *friend*. Then there are words that give auditory pleasure or are just lovely to say. *Plum. Assuage. Luminary*. These examples may well illustrate how personal the choices are when we think of our favourite words and that there are stories behind every one.

By crafting a series of lessons around favourite words you will be building on a resource in which your students have already made an emotional investment. Start by asking your class to share their favourite words. Once the students have noted them down, they should be encouraged to share them and to tell stories about why they are favourites. This can be done in pairs or small groups and to stimulate listening and class discussion, students should report back on other people's favourites. The point here is to be exploring the emotional connections that we have with language and implicitly this is a matter of understanding inference and connotation.

Plum, for instance is a lovely word to say. The plosive seems to be a satisfying sound to make and it's such a short word to say with a defined beginning and ending, the entirety of it is wrapped up perfectly in sound. Plums connote September, fading sunshine and the last days of wearing summer clothes before scarves come back out. The delicious, juicy burst of biting in to a ripe plum is one of life's lovely moments and it's hard for a teacher of English to think of a plum without recalling William Carlos Williams' 'This is just to say'.[1] Finally, one of the authors has very personal recollections of a Saturday job when he was a boy, sweeping a yard that happened to have a plum tree on one side. There was something wonderful about gorging on plums that day when he should have been working.

For your work with students on this topic, it will be valuable to explore all of the reasons why particular words are favourites. It's amazing how revealing it can be, how much you can share about yourselves in the classroom. Once this sharing has taken place, the students will be ready to explore the grammatical consequences and opportunities of favourite words.

Three simple sentence stems will help to get things started, with completed examples as suggestions.

(......) is my favourite word because ...
(......) makes other words better too. For instance ...
(......) isn't always a favourite word. Alongside ...

Plum is my favourite word because [see above].
Plum makes other words better too. For instance, 'I love my newly decorated bedroom, the purple walls are the best!' isn't nearly as good as the replacement 'the plum walls'.
Plum isn't always a favourite word. Alongside the word *bruise* and the image of decay, the word plum seems very different. 'A few days after being hit by the rounders ball, Roya's bruise was as tender as a nearly rotted plum.'

By undertaking these short pieces of writing, the students are developing their personal relationship with language, expressing their views, considering the best combination of word selection and word order and finally, they will be experimenting with how as writers, they can manipulate meanings through playing with the relationship between language and context.

There is innate value in this work, and perhaps combining it with other approaches to writing, it will have even greater potential to feature as part of a growing toolkit upon which your budding grammarians can draw.

Note

1   William Carlos Williams, available at www.poetryfoundation.org/poem/245576

Idea 10

Syntax

Every time we write or say something longer than a single word, we are applying syntactical understanding. Syntax is the field of linguistics dealing with word order and this section is about enabling and supporting your students to make the best choices consciously.

We are very familiar with commonly used sequences of words. Try it with the class. Ask which words could follow:

Happy
Car
Table

There are such common phrases that start with these words, it's likely that *birthday*, *park* and *cloth* will be given as suggestions. This isn't necessarily a bad thing, in fact that commonness forms part of cementing shared cultural experiences through language. For writers, being conscious of common phrases is important and seeking to avoid them in writing and speech is important. Your students need to be able to craft original phrases to be skilled users of their language.

There are conventions that determine our syntactic choices. At its most simple, this order is subject–verb–object, as in 'Animals breathe oxygen.' Beyond this there are other conventions that we follow unthinkingly such as reference to place coming before time, as in 'We break up from school on Friday.' Knowing these conventions means that your students can both adhere to them for sense and deviate from them for effect. Analyse the difference between:

We will be going on holiday in July.
In July, we will be going on holiday.
On holiday in July we will be going.

The first example follows the conventions of subject–verb–object and putting place first. The second version prioritises time, making July the dominant element. The third puts the same words in an intelligible form, though it is so far from being conventional that the syntax distracts from the sense. Using examples from texts already written, either by professional writers or your students, get the class to experiment with these three versions of a sentence.

Syntax is essentially about sequencing of ideas, and controlling that sequence gives the writer some control over the reader or audience response. This is the time to hand over this work to the class, and by giving some stimulus you can inspire understanding of the importance of word order. Tell the class they are going to create some marketing materials for something that is familiar to them; let's say your school. You could insist that some content is non-negotiable though there is complete freedom over how they write. Non-negotiables could include the lessons, the building and the lunches.

By starting with some thinking about sentences to describe the three key areas, students can rehearse how they would describe the lunches.

> The lunches are served in the main hall so we all get to eat together.
> We all eat together in the main hall at lunch time.

These versions of who eats lunch and when are very different. The first prioritises location, the second prioritises the communality of lunchtime. This gives a contrast between a very pragmatic description that would give the reader knowledge of where lunch occurs and a social focus that would show the reader that relationships are built and developed at meal times. Neither is better for they simply serve different purposes but by working through this students will become increasingly alert to nuanced effects of syntactic choices.

Dictionaries

The first dictionary of the English language was Cawdrey's *Table Alphabetical of Hard and Unusual Words*, published in 1604. It was a list of those words that Cawdrey felt were in need of explanation. As such, the first dictionary was not an attempt to include all the words of the language.

The format of dictionaries has developed over the years. Johnson's dictionary of 1755 was an early attempt to include all the words in the language. Dictionaries became an authoritative place to go to find out definitions and spellings. More recently, the Oxford English Dictionary is a historical version of the language. Once a word makes it into the OED it stays there whether it is in current parlance or not.

Over the years, there have been all sorts of interesting dictionaries that your students could explore. One such dictionary is the *Dictionary of the Vulgar Tongue* of 1811.[1] Bob Cromie writing in his introductory remarks to the 1971 US edition commented:

> An entertaining insight into the slang, wit and humor of late 18th and early 19th century England, when a 'Flaybottomist' was a school teacher, a 'Carrion Hunter' an undertaker, and a 'Buttock Broker' a matchmaker. Many words had different meanings then – 'High Living' meant 'to live in a garret or cockloft,' a 'Faggot' was a stand-in soldier and, with special apologies to today's feminists, 'To Lib' meant 'to lie together.' And, believe it or not, a 'Pig' was a policeman.

You can make a very entertaining list of expressions from this dictionary (although you will have to do the editing as there is some pretty rude stuff in there!). Here are some examples:

DIVER	A pickpocket; also one who lives in a cellar
HUCKLE MY BUFF	Beer, egg, and brandy, made hot
LICKSPITTLE	A parasite, or talebearer
RED RAG	The tongue; shut your potatoe trap, and give your red rag a holiday

There is much fun and thinking to be had from investigating how words have developed from their origins. Many of our words have been coined in literature. Take, for example, the word 'chortle'.

> **Chortle** v. chuckle or snort with glee. 1872, coined by Lewis Carroll in *Through the Looking Glass*, a blend of chuckle and snort. –n. 1903, from the verb.

You could be reading from the book and stop to investigate the word.

Chortle exemplifies one of the ways that we make new words, a blend.

motor and hotel – motel
motor and pedal – moped
jeans and leggings – jeggings
spoon and fork – spork
shorts and skirt – skort
Labrador and poodle – labradoodle

You could make an anthology of extracts that have words of interest in them. Or in the texts that you are already looking through you could search for words that have an interesting etymology to be explored.

Investigating vocabulary in these ways can really deepen a student's appreciation of the functions and roots of language. A history and context for vocabulary can lead to an articulacy around the use of words. Hopefully, the more you expose your students to a rich range of vocabulary the more competent they will become in making their own selections.

Note

1   *The Dictionary of the Vulgar Tongue*, 1812. Available at www.gutenberg.org/ebooks/5402

Stop PEE-ing!

Do you think that it would be interesting if all sentences were the same length? Average sentences in the English language are shorter than these ones, with fifteen words each. What is the impact on a reader of everything being the same number of words? Will they get into a rhythm that eventually gets a bit boring for that reader? We think that you would soon be tired if that happened all of the time. You would begin to crave something a bit different after a short while.

Argghhh! It becomes draining to read. The pattern is set and repeated. A reader might not notice that this is the problem with the writing but it will drain away their interest nonetheless.

And by extension, what if you were marking a set of student essays and they each used exactly the same structural technique throughout their writing? Point/Evidence/Explanation has become overused, to the point that it has become more important to include than the things that you actually have to say.

The PEE structure has made so much of the written product of students formulaic to the point of becoming indistinguishable from the work of their peers. Its original use was for supporting the work of students working towards a GCSE who were achieving grades around D. The hope was that this kind of scaffolding would support those students towards gaining a C grade. Schools have made its application much broader.

This has real implications for students aiming at the very highest grades. The mark schemes of exam boards require engagement and originality in their top-band descriptors. This is hard to achieve when your writing follows the same structural design as everyone else in your class. Higher achieving students who make use of the PEE structure tend to lose that aspect of writing that marks them out – flair.

In posing essay style questions is it possible for you to offer different routes through the planning of the essay? The thinking about the construction of essays needs to be around what a student has to say rather than the structure into which they will fit points.

Let's look at an example. Here is a question for planning.

Who is most responsible for the downfall of Antony; Enobarbus, Cleopatra or Antony himself?

This question most obviously suggests a three part approach, looking at the responsibility of each character listed in the question. Alternatively, your student might organise their essay around the reasons for Antony's downfall and suggest where responsibility might lie. The art of structuring the essay answer needs to come from the purpose of the essay. The essay needs to have something to say. What, in this instance, does the student think is the direct answer to the question? The direct answer will form the basis of the conclusive remarks and the rest of the essay will create an incremental sequence of paragraphs that leads to the end point. The selection of quotation and textual evidence should back up the line of enquiry taken. The freshest, most engaged writing will not have the evident repetitious PEE structure foregrounded.

Idea 13

Significance and value

We found a spelling test on the floor of a school in South Yorkshire (Figure 13.1). It makes us sad each time that we look at it.

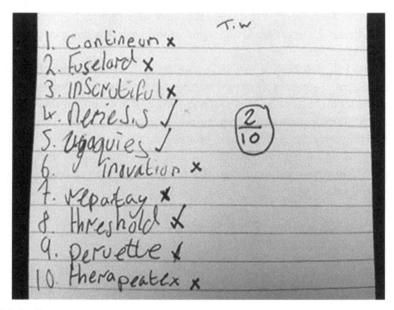

Figure 13.1 Spelling test

What can the teacher have been thinking? There is so much that is wrong here. When we test children there must be a built-in level of sense of achievement. No one should be going away with a score of 2/10 having marked their own answers without even being asked to write the correct answers out. If that happens, then inevitably, as has happened in this case, the test paper ends up on the floor.

The value of the test to the teacher is nil; they haven't kept a record of the scores or of the incorrect spellings. They don't know how the child has done so they can't build on the work that, presumably, was done in preparation for this test. The fact that it is on a scrap of paper indicates the throwaway nature of the activity and perhaps indicates the lack of importance the teacher attributes here. This test has no formative value and serves no summative purpose either. The teacher is no further along in their attempts to help their student.

The value of the test to the child is worse than nothing. The test confirms, to that child, that they have failed at spelling. You can see from reading the attempted spellings that the vocabulary is out of reach for this child. T.W. is not going to want to share his/her result and he/she will come to the activity next time with less confidence than this.

When you construct testing it needs to have a sense of importance to the child taking the test. How will you sell the test to the children in your class? Why would they want to take the test? In what ways will they be richer for the experience of learning for, and then taking, the test? What is the value of your test? These things need to be explicit in learning. If your student knows that there is something significant about a test then they will more readily prepare for it and be better motivated to demonstrate the best that they can do. We agree that this is nothing new or profound but are you sure that you always indicate the importance and value of the tests that you put in front of the students?

T.W. needs a test that he/she can achieve more in. The teacher needs to know the current capacity of the child and design testing that is suitable for growing the confidence of the student. If this test is part of a sequence of testing then the students need to feel that they have a chance of achieving in the next test.

Tests of grammatical knowledge must be stopping off points as your students make progress towards becoming fully competent and articulate communicators in speech and writing. If your tests are capturing part of that development then they will have significance and value.

Exploding sentences

Children often write very functional sentences. If you ask most children to write you a story, they will think long and hard about the plot and characters but will hardly consider the construction of the writing itself. Plot tends to be driven by what happens. Expression and punctuation are the last concerns in their heads and on their plans when they are developing their ideas. This can lead to some uninteresting writing, even when the idea for the story is a good one.

Your students need to be reminded often of the need for the writing to be interesting if a reader is to enjoy the story/article etc. Exploding sentences is one way that this can be achieved.

Here is a sequence of functional sentences that a student might write.

The door opened and he went inside. He looked around. The room was big.

This is the sort of writing that students might produce when they are focused on the plot of their stories. We think that they are transcribing for you the cinematic action that is taking place in their mind's eye. They see the story as a mix of their imagination; based on contemporary tv/film structures, video game scenarios and the range, and limitations, of their imagination. The writing is centred on plot and a sense of the writer 'seeing' the situation that the character finds themself in. When students are writing in this way, they tend to choose 'everyday' vocabulary because of their focus on detailing plot.

With a group, you could introduce the idea of exploding sentences. You want your students to blow up the sentences to make them more dramatic. You want the writer to remember that the reader needs to have the best possible idea of not just what is happening but also the atmosphere and the ways in which characters are feeling and reacting to the situations in the story. It is possible to explode sentences to improve the enjoyment of the reader.

For example, how would the story change if we replaced *The* door with *A* door? Discuss together the way in which the move from the definite article to the indefinite article adds to the mystery of the place. The technical vocabulary need not appear in the discussion first time round. Perhaps later. Perhaps when the students begin to examine their own drafts we could have a 'sift and sort' activity to separate the two types, once we have the idea of the general and the particular nature of these words. The importance of knowing whether an article is definite or indefinite is limited to developing an appreciation of the benefits of employing one rather than the other. When is it best to be definite and when best to be more general? This is the move from declarative knowledge to procedural knowledge. Declarative knowledge feeds procedural knowledge.

How would the story change if we described how the door opened: *slowly, easily, quietly, abruptly*. Make selections. Change the selections. Test drive words that might enhance the quality of the writing. Remind the students of the need to think about audience and purpose. They also need to think about the type of writing they are trying to achieve. If the story is to make the reader scared/sad/laugh, how is this being achieved?

What if we got rid of *and*? How could we bring the two parts of that first sentence together? Is there a punctuation mark that we could use? Could we add any words to the sentences that would improve the reader's experience? Can we break up the use of consistently short sentences? If we find ways of making the three sentences one sentence, does this improve the writing?

In-depth analysis, modelled by you is a good starting point to getting the students to then find sentences that they want to work on in their own writing.

Making the exploding of sentences a routine – a norm – in your classroom will make it more effective than just trying it once, or now and again. Make it a part of the drafting process. Sometimes you might decide to devote a portion of the lesson to exploding sentences. On other occasions, it might just be a whisper in the ear of the student who has come to you to say that they are finished with their writing.

Students in this digital age are used to instant gratification and their sense of the pace of communication is faster than an adult might find acceptable. This does have the side effect that students want to be done and dusted with writing even more than in the past. If they are working on computers to produce their work, we think that students can sometimes think that drafting has been replaced by the correction functions on the screen. These, of course, deal with errors of standard spelling, punctuation and grammar rather than the aesthetic qualities of a piece of writing. Students need to be encouraged to think about the quality of their writing and exploding sentences offers a detailed review, sentence by sentence.

Grammar working wall

Grammar is a broad term and grammatical understanding does not happen immediately. It is important to deliberately craft a long-term approach to developing your pupils' confidence. This will allow for understanding to grow and develop as well as creating opportunities to learn from mistakes.

A grammar working wall can be a place where the progress to understanding gets logged and supported. It can be a place where mistakes are celebrated, peer teaching is enacted and diagnosis to inform planning happens.

A working wall is a classroom display that celebrates work in progress. It's not a display of neatly copied out 'best' work. Working walls are already a feature of many classrooms, so this section may simply adapt something that is already part of your practice, though it may introduce something new.

Create a resource of new, difficult and ambitious words that you think your students are unlikely to know. They should be from different word classes, ideally they may be words that function as more than one type. A suggested list could come from Table 15.1. Show the list to the class and ask them to write sentences including the new vocabulary. You'll quickly have a bank of sentences and can move on to explore the choices that your young writers have created.

What would you do with the sentence, 'To help them to make more windows, the company bought three quixotics'? There is a clear understanding that quixotic could work as a noun and an explanation might be that when heard aloud, quixotic sounds like a blending of quick and robotic, so the company had invested in three new machines that would increase the rate of production. To be able to write this sentence, a student would have demonstrated their innate ability to apply grammatical conventions, they have creatively predicted a meaning (incorrectly!) and will have justified their decision to put words in a certain order. This is engaging stuff and embeds talk and learning about grammar in an appealing way.

You will also have a huge resource to create the first version of your grammar working wall. Sentences can be written on to sheets of paper with space left for annotations. Get them stuck up on the wall and you have the beginning of an interactive space for peer teaching and learning. To stimulate the activity, a few questions will support focused interaction.

- What does the writer think this word means?
- How have they used the word in their sentence?
- Can you improve the sentence in any way?

This loose structure for interaction is the beginning of grammatical discussions being commonplace and the wall can continue to be a vibrant, exploratory place. For future resources to keep the wall alive, you may use photocopied versions of students' writing, extracts from any published text, texts that focus on this half-term's topic. The important thing is that the wall becomes a space for commentary and explanations, analysis and explorations.

As part of your diagnostic toolkit, the wall also works as a means for you to understand the areas of strength and development in your students. This will inform planning which should, of course, include new activities on the grammar wall.

Table 15.1

quixotic	nefarious	quince	rhombus
circadian	formalin	gossamer	isotope
baize	actuate	osseous	spondee
travois	vulcanise	internist	hyrax
dolmen	mucilage	liminal	promontory

Finding your voices – auto/biography

We all need stories if we are to live fulfilled lives. We need to tell stories and we need to hear stories for they form the foundation of human relationships.

Stories are common currency in schools and classrooms and pupils are experienced users of a range of styles of storytelling. Factual stories to illuminate historical events or scientific exploration are as likely heard as recounts of weekend experiences or works of fiction. Developing storytelling is an opportunity to enhance natural ability and desire to interact with and create our world through relationships.

It is as common for pupils to want to tell personal stories as it is for teachers to use autobiography as a means to enable self-expression. Autobiography can seem like a tempting mode of writing as all pupils have a story to tell. We know how difficult it can be to make oneself sound interesting, however, just remember the hours spent paining over a cover letter for a job application and the pupils' claims that they don't know what to write seems very real. Autobiography, then, is a case of how to write, not what, and how to write is a case for grammar.

In this section we will consider the relationships between autobiography, biography and narrative fiction. At its simplest, the difference between the styles of writing can be a difference in pronouns. Changing a sentence from 'I wanted to study physics before I discovered a love of poetry' to 'She wanted to study Physics until discovering a love of poetry' marks the shift between autobiography and biography, or between first person and third person narrative fiction. The point is that when your students can articulate and manipulate the effect of switching pronouns they are becoming competent grammarians.

Let's assume that your pupils have produced autobiographical writing before and that by revisiting it we are creating the opportunity to refine a skill through conscious manipulation of grammar. So start small and in a way that you know the children in your class will enjoy. One model that works is interview triads. In groups of three, ascribe interviewer, interviewee and note-taker roles. Set tight limits on the scope of the interview. It should focus on a single event, like the walk to school or going somewhere for the first time.

The class should be set up to tell details that embellish the tale, not to cram it full of events. Modelling this approach will demonstrate the roles as well as creating opportunities for questioning. You could even create a bank of rich questions together as a class.

If you act as interviewee and pupils act as interviewer and scribe, you can conduct a five-minute interview for the class and they will see the level of detail required in the respondent's answers. Alternatively three students could take the roles and you could stop the discussion for some real time analysis of the conversation. The activity can be rotated three times so that all pupils experience all three roles, or for brevity's sake it could be done once and the pupils use the same source material.

Once every pupil has a set of notes from which to craft a piece of writing the next stage of learning can begin. There are various ways to undertake this phase of the lesson, and the children remain in their working triads. Here are two models.

- All pupils write their own paragraph or two of autobiographical writing. You will encourage the application of skills as relevant to your pupils, be it sentence structure, descriptive language or anything else. There's no need to be explicit about pronouns at this stage, just see what happens.
- The pupils each take a different style and write the story in their given form. The interviewee writes autobiography, interviewer writes biography and the scribe writes fiction.

The groups now have a resource to analyse the function of pronouns in personal writing. Using the ideas in Idea 3 (on marginal commentaries), the students can now either reflect on their own writing or a peer's and you can steer the focus to pronouns. During the writing activity you or a colleague can write the paragraphs from the modelled conversation to provide material for the next part of the lesson.

There are many ways to measure the effectiveness of this, and we would offer that using spoken presentations would be the most valuable. If one group read the versions of the story aloud to the class and shared their insights on the ways that pronouns work, as part of a wider piece of analysis, it reinforces grammar as part of classroom discourse rather than an isolated element of learning. It also invites discussion and input from other students. Once this has happened once or twice as a whole class, further presentations and discussions can be shared between triads.

Handwriting

It is interesting to reflect on the fact that we all have a unique style of handwriting. Even identical twins who share appearance and genetics don't have the same handwriting. They are like fingerprints; some people may be able to copy them, but they will never be the same.

Some aspects of handwriting seem to be pre-determined. If you are left- or right-handed it may well have an impact upon how you make the strokes of your letters. For instance, let's look at the forming of a capital *A*. If you are right-handed you will probably start at the bottom of the formation and work up. If you are left-handed, however, you are more likely to start at the top of the formation and work down. This has less to do with your hands and more to do with your brain. The brain tells the hand what to do.

This puts the attempts of schools to work on handwriting into a different light.

Here are some characteristics of handwriting that you and your students might think about as you look to make script as clear as is possible:

- specific shape of letters, e.g. their roundness or sharpness;
- regular or irregular spacing between letters;
- the slope of the letters;
- the rhythmic repetition of the elements;
- the pressure to the paper;
- the average size of letters;
- the thickness of letters.

There is fun to be had in asking students to write with their 'unfamiliar' hand, or even their feet. This exercise will demonstrate to them that they have developed a skill in writing with their 'familiar' hand (however negatively they feel about the presentation of their writing). It will also demonstrate the problems that a baby had when presented with pencils and crayons. Your students can experiment with the best ways to hold a pen. They can become critical friends, observing each other as they write. The critical friend can be offering tips and observations around what they see.

As a class, we think that it is important that you lead the group to the understanding that there is a range of acceptable and attractive handwriting styles. The point of 'neat' handwriting is that the reader is able to read the ideas of the writer as they intended, without having to figure out what the squiggles on the page actually say. Once that happens then the momentum is lost.

Writing for real audiences

Schools can be abstract places at times. Much of what we ask students to do there is removed from their lives outside the school gates. Often when we ask students to write, it is because we want to develop their capacities in the activity of writing itself. Writing for its own sake. In this circumstance, there is a danger that the sense of writing having an audience can be lost. Often the students are writing to no one with the express purpose of proving that they can write. Curious!

I think that we need to remember that the main types of writing that students are doing outside of school no longer involve paper and pen. They are interacting through messaging their friends by text, updating and responding to Facebook statuses, and tweeting on Twitter amongst other forms of keeping in touch and informed. Short, informal communications each with their own set of conventions; conventions that your students have learnt for themselves without the apparatus of schools. Our students write much more than previous generations of students over the course of a normal day. Their desire to be instantly and constantly connected is a new development caused by the potential of the technologies in their pockets. Writing with paper and pen is one of those things that increasingly distances school from the 'real' world of communication.

Can we invite this 'real' world into schools?

It is interesting that young people are writers in ways that previous generations couldn't even have dreamt about. Yet students do not always value the communications that they make as 'writing' and feel that they are not writers. Perhaps this is partly due to the distance that schools place between themselves and the ways that the young actually write. Will you embrace the worldwide audience that might potentially read the work of your students?

Increasing numbers of young people express themselves through writing blogs. Blogs are easy to set up. Your teaching could very easily encompass blogging. Could homework take the form of a blog sometimes, in place of more traditional forms of exercise book writing? Exam boards used to frown on the idea of blogs, with chief examiners reporting that the audience was difficult to judge. It is difficult to let this misgiving stand these days. Your students understand the nature of blogging and make use of it with a clear sense of the parameters of the form.

Moving away from the internet, the real world around the students offers myriad audiences. The student comes with all sorts of social groupings who would be pleased to read the writing of one from among their group. There will be groups that could benefit from the writing of your students. If you have a student who helps out at his/her local tennis club kiddies sessions, do you think that the club would value your student writing a new leaflet for the tennis professional to take into schools to promote the Saturday morning lessons? Surely the impetus behind the writing of the student will only gather momentum when they perceive what they are doing to be important and practical

Real audiences, whether provided by you or by the student themselves, have needs. Genuine writing often needs to suit the audience rather than the writer. This is a good lesson for young writers to learn. Sometimes you have to write to order rather than what you fancy doing/saying.

Chasing the dream

Teachers enable children and young people to achieve their dreams. Sometimes this happens directly and at others it is the continuous work undertaken by any teachers that enables young people to be ready to enter the adult world. Primary school teachers foster a love of learning and a co-operative spirit in their pupils that readies them for secondary school. Secondary school teachers continue that process, enabling young people to gain the qualifications they need to be successful. All of this is a massive responsibility and of course, this is not the experience of school for all children and young people; some are less fortunate.

In order for us to fulfil the ultimate responsibility that we accept when signing a teaching contract we need to know our students' aspirations. Knowing those aspirations is the first step to being able to support them being reached. This section is a suggestion about how to learn about those hopes and dreams for the future.

The starting point needs to be regular discussions about the world of work, to include broad discussions about what lies beyond the school and more detailed investigations into which qualifications and experiences are required to get a dream job. This could be an activity that becomes a regular task, a regular morning discussion or a golden time activity with primary school pupils. Equally it could be a regular feature of English lessons in secondary schools, or a little planning between tutor teams and the English department could make it a morning activity that starts in tutor time and is developed in English lessons.

From there, the discussion needs to be tailored towards specific writing tasks. These will take various forms and could include:

- writing a letter seeking an experience that would be a step towards gaining a dream job;
- writing a job description for a dream job;
- writing a letter of application;
- creating a recruitment campaign to inspire interest in a job or field of work.

The final written products will all require some analysis of existing versions of these texts. It is always interesting to analyse a teacher's job description with students – they'll start to see just how much you do beyond teaching lessons! Undertaking analysis, some modelling and a scaffold or two will ensure that your students will be able to write well about a subject they have chosen themselves.

In terms of the writing itself, whichever form you choose, specific grammatical techniques can be emphasised. Informative language can be enhanced by switching between impersonal and personal voice. For instance, 'Designing and building houses can change the world for the better. There is nothing that I would like more than to be an architect.' In this pair of sentences the impersonal statement about building is then complemented by the personal perspective. Similarly, brevity in sentence construction can make language persuasive. In fact, readers demand it in today's time-pressured and visual culture. The simple sentence, 'Build lives' as a headline, or even the only text in an online advert to recruit undergraduates to an architecture degree course demonstrates great skill as a writer.

Of course teaching grammatical tricks and skills is important. It will help students on their way to becoming proficient and confident linguists. However, this approach to teaching grammar opens up rich conversations about why that proficiency is important and puts you in the driving seat to guide and develop your students' learning in the right direction to ensure they have every opportunity to fulfil their aspirations.

Telling stories

Humans are the storytelling animals. We need to make sense of our experiences and to communicate our thoughts and feelings; storytelling is so often the medium through which we choose to do this. It seems to be something that comes to us quite instinctively. If someone asks you what you did at the weekend or what was the proudest moment of your life, you can quickly gather together the characters, settings and plot required and set out on entertaining and/or informing your audience. Our skill is such that it can become quite easy to overlook that skill.

There is certainly merit in taking time with your students to examine how we construct stories. Perhaps you could get students to record each other telling stories. Groups could then look at different aspects of the story telling craft.

Here are some aspects of storytelling that your students could go looking for (a limited list to get you thinking!):

- How do we open stories? What are the techniques we use to engage the reader/listener? How do we let the reader/listener get the contextual detail that they need to get going with the story? In speech there is often much frontloading of contextual detail to give the listener the information about character and plot before the main body of the plot begins. For example: 'I guess it was last week because it was (.) the night before my (.) birthday and Sam, from the builder's merchants had just been round (3) anyway Rob's sister turns up unannounced like (.) which was strange because...' Your group could look at how written stories go about this process of informing the reader in the opening pages. They will probably observe a good deal of difference from the opening of spoken stories.
- A group could look at the language surrounding the climax/exciting parts of the storytelling. Is there a dominant word class at these points? Is there a type of word that is used more often in these parts than in other parts of a story? What about sentence length/utterance length?
- Ask your students to try to write in different genres. Once they have begun/had a go then get them to analyse what the features are of different types of writing. Can they identify any grammatical structures/vocabulary choices that are used in certain contexts?
- What are the different ways of introducing characters to a story? Do you always

have to describe their appearance? How do you describe a person's appearance and distinguish them from anyone else?

- How do you write dialogue/conversation in a story so that it feels realistic? Do you always need the *said person A/said person B* formula? How do you make it clear who is speaking without using *he said/she said*?
- How do you choose the right vocabulary for younger audiences? Perhaps you could make use of a Fry Graph here. The Fry Graph is a measurement of the average sentence length and the average number of syllables per one hundred words. These measurements are then plotted on the Fry Graph to give a reading age/score. This is a practical way for students to measure whether the writing that they are aiming at a particular audience has the right level of demand. They will be able to tell whether the vocabulary is too challenging/too easy or whether they need to extend/shorten the length of their sentences. We think that this activity does make students reflect on the quality of their writing, as well as the content.

Thinking through the construct of a story and the requirements of types of writing is important in creating a thoughtful writer, one that is alert to the needs of audience as well as what they have to say. You will know that presented with the chance to write anything, students tend to be full of the needs of what they want to say and can often reach for the first words that come into their minds. Crafting writing needs a slower, more thoughtful process based on an informed understanding of audience and purpose.

Twitter stories

You can begin this activity with a recap about 'What is a story?' Take the opportunity to unlock prior learning by leading a discussion or group activity to gain a shared understanding of what makes a certain piece of writing a narrative. The following list is not exhaustive though should offer a decent list of important elements.

- a series of events that are retold by a participant or an observer;
- a text that tells of events that real people or invented characters were involved in;
- a text that is designed to entertain the reader;
- a structured recount of inter-related events;
- a story needs characters, places, events – a plot;
- there may be deeper elements, like themes, that drive the narrative.

For the purposes of differentiation it is the identification of these elements that is important, the vocabulary to explain them can be developed as the lessons continue. As a final word on how this initial thinking can be gathered, it may also be interesting to experiment with setting the task as homework. Your students could then undertake independent research by asking family members, thinking through with friends or looking online.

Twitter stories as examples

These stories combine many of the elements above in the confines of the 140-character limit that Twitter allows. To develop the thinking that has come from the homework or discussions around 'What is a story?' the students should start to identify the narrative elements that have been used and then use that identification to analyse narrative effects. Here are some guiding questions to move identification of techniques to narrative analysis.

- Do you care about what happens to the character/s?
- How might this story make a reader feel?
- How has the writer got a sense of time in to their story?
- What might have happened before or after the events in this story?
- Could you make the story better?

Again, the list is not exhaustive and the questions that you pose will be determined by the level of your students' prior understanding.

What follows are two alternative approaches to teaching your students to craft a 140-character story. They can be built up from the very shortest sentence or can be pared down from a longer text.

Writing a Twitter story – version I

The shortest viable sentence we can write is made up of two words, a noun and a verb. *Crocodiles bite. Robert cried. Melissa jogged.* Even these sentences have meanings that can be inferred. We are warned of the dangers of crocodiles and it is clear that we should steer clear of them. Something has caused Robert to experience an outpouring of emotion and Melissa may be late, or keeping fit.

The next step is to build a story. There will be many false starts and mistakes. There will be great ideas that have to be saved for another day and there will be great successes. There needs to be regular counting and lots of editing. The process and final products will be better if the students have talked through their stories as they go, read them out loud and taken ideas from their peers.

In the following examples the number of characters used is indicated in brackets:

Melissa jogged. (15)

From this starting point the story needs a location.

Melissa jogged across the meadow. (33)

Adding a location gives the story a sense of place and by retaining the simple sentence structure we have given ourselves some freedom to play with structure in my next attempt.

To clear her head, Melissa jogged across the meadow. (52)

Deliberately turning this in to a complex sentence gives Melissa a character beyond being a jogger. Something has happened and there is an emerging sense of mystery.

After that, Melissa needed to clear her head. Jogging helps so she headed for the meadow. (89)

I liked the sense of mystery, and to develop it the sentence structures needed to change. Choosing the word 'that' at the beginning of the story increases uncertainty in the reader, makes Melissa's situation increasingly mysterious and keeps the complex sentence opener. This move has also enabled more characterisation. The phrase 'Jogging helps' implies that Melissa has had troubled times before and she runs to think things through.

'I'll never forget. Or forgive. I hate you.' After that, Melissa needed to clear her head. Jogging helps so she headed for the meadow. (131)

The story needed speech and we have deliberately not stated who says the words. Are they spoken by or to Melissa? There is now passion and upset. There's a reason for the escape to the meadow. Excitingly, we are nearly at my character limit too but have another idea to work in. We want to show that Melissa is crying.

'I'll never forget. Or forgive. I hate you.' After that, Melissa needed to clear her head. Jogging helps so she headed for the meadow as her face wettened. (152)

This has put us over the limit, partly because of wanting to show that Melissa is crying rather than tell the reader. It needs to be pared down.

'I'll never forget. Or forgive. I hate you.' After that, Mel needed to clear her head. Jogging helps. She headed for the meadow; her face wettened. (140)

And it's there! Losing 12 characters wasn't too tricky and it has arguably improved the story. Mel feels more familiar than Melissa, using a two-word sentence sharpens the pace and replacing 'as' with a semi-colon creates a more appropriate voice for a 140-character story.

Writing a Twitter story – version 2

Simply make a longer text shorter. Your students could either write, storyboard or tell their story aloud and then start reducing and condensing it down to 140 characters.

> Melissa and her mum hadn't been getting on at all well. It all goes back to when her Grandma was in hospital. Everyone was finding it difficult to cope, and Melissa found it especially hard to accept the way her mum was treating Grandma. The day that they screamed at each other in the hospital car park is still a raw memory and is still causing tension. Melissa regrets saying that she'll never forgive her mum, but couldn't apologise, not yet. She needed to sort her own head out before trying to fix the relationship with her mum. The only thing that she knew would help would be to go jogging in the meadow – her refuge in tough times.

Here is a one-paragraph story that could well have been the source of the final Twitter story above. There is some contextual information about Melissa's family situation, there is the chance to add some detail about people and places and because of the greater word limit, it's possible for the narrator to embellish everything.

Paring this down really is challenging work. Simply cutting words and sentences will get the character limit down, but it will be impossible to retain the depth of character-isation and narrative. It's also tough because the students will have to abandon some of their thinking. To get this down to the limit the reference to Grandma has to go, the history of the mother/daughter relationship has to go and the hospital setting too. Most challenging, and where the grammatical learning takes place, is restructuring sentences to retain the sense whilst losing words.

I would suggest that to do this, using a highlighter to identify the absolutely vital parts that must be retained, which could leave us with 'difficult', 'screamed', 'jogging' and 'refuge'. Now that there are two resources, the full story and the essence of it in four words, crafting can begin.

With both of these ideas, the ultimate aim is to produce publishable stories that can be shared online. This can be done safely on Twitter, where accounts can be set up so that only accepted contacts can comment. It might be that you can showcase these texts through the school's account.

Just because it is

How do languages actually function? Who decides when a word is a word and what that word is going to mean? How do new words make it in to the language? There are moments that we can pinpoint when certain people and events had influence over the shape of our language. For instance, the Norman invasion of 1066 left us with over 20,000 borrowings from the French language. The introduction of the King James Authorised Bible of 1611 to every church in the land meant that the words spoken within it became very influential.

However, the truth of the matter is that language is not really an entity, it is a thing that we do. No one person or authority is in charge of how a language will develop. Languages change and adapt to meet the needs of the people that speak that language. Each generation fashions the language to suit its needs. In that sense language is very democratic. We all have a say in how we will express ourselves.

The English language is one that has many irregularities. This is due, in part, because of the large number of influences that have been brought to bear upon it; Anglo-Saxon, Norse, Viking, French and more recently global influences. Over the 1500 years or so of our language's existence, the spelling and meaning of vocabulary and the grammatical structures into which we put those words have adapted many times and at differing rates in different places. Languages are symptomatic of their users.

In English, we, the speakers, have made some tacit agreements about how the language works. Unspoken understandings of meaning.

There is fun to be had with your students around the idiosyncratic elements to our language. Here are just three examples.

- You could set them off on a hunt for idioms. Idioms are expressions in which the words create a meaning past their literal definitions. For example, 'She was wet so they left her out in the cold' or similarly, 'They sent her to Coventry.' Experienced users of the language could identify the meaning of these expressions but it must be hard for a non-native speaker to start to build an understanding of such expressions. We are sure that your students will be able to pick out loads of these expressions. You could have an idioms board/display in your classroom – a working space to which the students keep adding.
- What about pairs of words that come in a 'natural' order. *Fish and chips* sounds

right whilst *chips and fish* does not. It is our custom to say the first and that makes it comfortable on the ear. Similarly, *vinegar and salt* and *Mrs and Mr* feel awkward. How many of these pairings can your students find?

- Adjectival order is another area of the language that works 'just because it is'. There are numerous websites that will try to instruct language users on the way to order adjectives in a sentence. However, each will also offer the fact that there are no hard and fast rules. One even suggests that you should ask a native speaker who will probably have a strong opinion about what is the correct practice. The truth of the matter is that none of us really know, or need to know, rules around this area of the language. We are capable, as mother tongue speakers, of finding the natural sounding options.

I think that it can be important to explore the rough edges of our language. Students become alert to the fact that following the 'rules' will only get you so far. After that point you meet the irregular and sometimes inexplicable. You can be overwhelmed and you can be underwhelmed, so why can't you just be whelmed?

Idea 23

New punctuation marks and emoticons

You may well have heard of the Sarcmark (see Figure 23.1).

Never again be misunderstood! Never again waste a good sarcastic line on someone who doesn't get it!

Sarcasm – Punctuate It – SarcMark

The official, easy-to-use punctuation mark to emphasize a sarcastic phrase, sentence or message. Once downloaded to your computer or cell phone, it's a quick key-stroke or two to insert the ว where you want, when you want, in your communications with the world.

Figure 23.1 The Sarcmark
Source: www.sarcmark.com

A new punctuation mark for a new digital age. It serves the function of making clear when you are being sarcastic, primarily when sending emails and phone messages. It replaces the look that you might have on your face when being sarcastic in a face-to-face conversation. Sarcasm doesn't always come across clearly in written text.

As you can perhaps tell from the language above, the Sarcmark was for sale; a downloadable punctuation mark for just one dollar ninety cents!

You could give the Sarcmark as an example of a made-up punctuation mark. Explore the function of the Sarcmark and see if your students think that its graphic form is suitable for the role it is to play in writing. Then you could invite your students to come up with a new punctuation mark of their own. This would involve thinking through the purpose/use of the new punctuation mark and then designing and drawing the symbol.

A similar activity that your students would enjoy is in coming up with new emoticons. Here, they make use of the punctuation marks on the keyboard to produce symbols that express feelings (see Figure 23.2 for some examples).

	Embarrassed	:-[		Confused	:-?
	Grin	:-D		Wink Tongue	;-P
	Tongue	:-P		Lips Are Sealed	:-X
	Crying	:'-(		Wink	;-)
	Shouting	>:-O		Kiss	:-*
	Evil	>:-D		Innocent	O:-)
	Angry	>:-(		Money Mouth	:-$
	Mischievous	>:-)		Smile	:-)
	Grinning Wink	;-D		Not Amused	>:-	
	Blushing	:-]		Angry Tongue	>:-P
	Oops	:-!		Frown	:-(
	Undecided	:-\		Cool	B-)
	Smirk	:->		Straight Faced	:-	
	Grimmace	X-(		Sleeping		-)
	Gasp	:-o			

Figure 23.2 Emoticons
Source: www.hacktrix.com

In approaching this activity you could show a few emoticons to get students thinking about what to do. If some are struggling to come up with their own ideas then you could give them the required feeling and ask them to invent an emoticon for that feeling.

Here is mine – the devilish grin   ;]

I know it isn't very good. But then, students sometimes like to do better than the teacher, especially when the teacher's attempt is so poor.

In designing new punctuation marks and new emoticons your students are thinking very specifically about the functions of symbols in language. Evidently, you want to develop the confidence that they have in writing extended sentences. Knowing how punctuation marks function is key to their abilities in creating complexity in their written structures. Having examined the functions of these made-up punctuation marks and emoticons, you can lead an exploration of the jobs done by the standard punctuation marks of standard written English.

You might extend this activity into a research project around when and where the various punctuation marks came from. For your students to understand that they arrived into the language at different times will be another way that you can help them understand that language is always changing.

Grammar t-shirts

Grammar t-shirts? What a fashion statement. Will they catch on? Could they become a joint project with the Textiles department? You have seen the grammar cartoons on Twitter and Facebook and the like. Could your students come up with designs that they could screen-print? You know the sort of thing (Figure 24.1).

Figure 24.1 Grammar t-shirt
Source: http://blog.writeathome.com/wp-content/uploads/2013/06/Grammar-Pirate1-300x232.jpg

Or, we could get some blank white t-shirts and use marker pens to design grammar t-shirts that have whatever rules we need on them. Then the students wear the t-shirts in lessons when we are focusing on grammar. When someone needs help with the apostrophe, over comes the kid with the apostrophe t-shirt on.

Your students will have to think through the design of the t-shirt. That will require them to come up with a design that clearly explains the point of grammar. Your students will be learning as they make the t-shirt and will benefit from the advice when it is made. The novelty of the t-shirt will support remembering the points of grammar on the designs. We know that your students could also make posters for the wall but we think the t-shirts will engage them a little more effectively.

Sorting out confusing words

Here is a list of pairings of words that will need to be sorted out by your students. Can you think through how your investigators are going to do this activity and how they will share their new found skill in sorting out the confusing words? Perhaps they could make some short instructional videos that you could then place on the school's shared drive.

affect – effect
anticipate – expect
ensure – insure
can – may
complement – compliment
dependant – dependent
empathy – sympathy
fair – fare
hanged – hung
lay – lie
should – would
stationary – stationery
that – which
who – whom

A quick search on the internet will reveal the answers to you if you are a bit iffy about any of these. We could tell you the answers here but we think that you will internalise the information better if you have to go looking for it yourself. We are sure that you can see that this will also apply to your students; you could spoon-feed them or they could do their own research. Again, the act of finding out can be handed over to the students. The act of thinking through the distinctions and usages can be handed over. The thinking about how to feedback to the class can be handed over.

High-frequency language

The Cambridge English Corpus is a collection of over one billion words in use, in both writing and in speech.[1] A corpus can tell us many interesting things about the way the language is actually employed. It can tell us the most frequently used words (in speech: *you, I, yeah, know, oh, okay, so it's, that's just, really, gonna/going to, right, we, think, well, mean, good, mm, stuff*), the day of the week that is mentioned the most (Friday) and can provide the contexts for how we actually use words. This can help us understand which of the many uses of a word with multiple applications is the one most used.

Here is a collection of the most frequent five word stretches in the English language. These combinations of five words appear more frequently than any other in English.

you know what I mean	as a matter of fact	what do you think about
I don't know if you	one of the things that	I think a lot of
at the end of the	there are a lot of	how do you feel about
in the middle of the	every once in a while	I don't know if I
I don't know what the	and that kind of thing	I was going to say
I know a lot of	and that sort of stuff	I think it would be
A lot of people that	we have a lot of	

What do your students notice about these stretches of five words? Are there patterns that they can spot? What does it say about the language? Can you get your students to write the words that they think regularly go around these stretches?

Students could be encouraged to put texts into Wordle formats that indicate the frequency with which words are used in a text (see Figure 26.1). Your students could guess the words that they think are going to be high frequency before they go into the Wordle. They could put their own writing into Wordle and see if the high-frequency vocabulary that they have used reflects the sorts of things that they hoped to write about. This could be a very useful analytical tool.

We are sure that your students will enjoy making Wordles. It is interesting to note the fact that the words can create a composite sense of meaning without the use of traditional punctuation marks.

Figure 26.1 Wordle
Source: www.wordle.net/

Note

1   See www.cambridge.org/br/about-us/what-we-do/cambridge-english-corpus

Broadening active vocabulary

Our active vocabulary is the words upon which we can draw and use with confidence. Words that we either commonly or irregularly use and always those that can be employed in speech or writing without consciously thinking it through.

To develop as confident users of their language, children and young people need to be taught and encouraged to broaden their active vocabulary. It will make them better communicators and will be an enabling skill that influences ability in all areas of the curriculum.

There are loads of good websites that have ideas, games and strategies to use in order to expand vocabulary. Searching through will mean that you can pick things, especially if it is games, that your students will like. Or get them to. However it happens, draw on the world of resources that are available online.

Beyond that, there are things that you can do in class that will support the importance of broadening vocabulary; here are three further ideas.

Ridiculous rewrites

Take a pre-written text – pretty much anything will work – and present it to the class. It can be fiction, non-fiction, something professionally created or something written by a student. Song lyrics can be effective too. Using this text as the foundation for playing around with vocabulary extension, set the class the text of changing it with a thesaurus. This can result in utterly transformed, often silly, nonsensical texts. For example, the first couple of sentences of Carol Klein's section on summer herbs, from her book *Cook Your Own Veg*, becomes the following text, with words changed through the indiscriminate use of a thesaurus italicised.[1]

> By summer, *cleansed* in *thick* sunshine, vegetables are *recoiled* to *evolve* their *stuffed taste*. The herbs we *employ* to *deepen* that *taste* in *frying* poised to embellish them, *exploding* with flavour, *wealthy* and redolent of the Mediterranean.

This isn't just about making silly new versions of texts. The discussions that follow the laughs will unlock how writers choose vocabulary that is relevant to audience and context. As you ask the pupils to explain their choices, you are creating the environment in which they become playful, curious and confident when manipulating their choices.

Word of the day/week/topic

Word walls are familiar to all classrooms, in fact in many they may well have become wallpaper. They don't need to be though, for in the best examples they are an active part of the room and brought in to the lessons by adults and children. This is the key to the success of this tool as a means to develop active vocabulary. The words on the wall need to be actively brought in to talk and writing and children celebrated for doing so.

Class discussions

Leading discussions with a whole class gives many students the chance to talk, share their views and test ideas out in public before committing them to paper. They also allow teachers to understand how well their students are understanding the material being discussed. It creates a space for growing and learning from others whilst for some, it creates anxiety or an opportunity to hide for a while.

The best discussions are convened by a teacher who then has the confidence to step back and allow their students to interact directly with each other rather than every comment being channelled through the teacher. When students are building on, or challenging each other's ideas, classroom talk is at its best. To intervene in this and use rich classroom talk as a means to expand vocabulary can be rewarding too. You can set up the discussion so that whenever someone makes a contribution, the next speaker has to make the same point but expressed differently. So if a student, in a discussion about *Private Peaceful* says that 'what happens to Tommo is horrible and unfair', the next contribution could be something like 'I agree, the way that Tommo is treated is unjust and makes me angry.' This recrafting of each other's utterances brings in vocabulary extension at a peer to peer level rather than through teacher-led instruction.

Fundamentally, helping students' vocabulary to grow needs to be fostered by a classroom culture that celebrates diversity of opinion alongside diversity of means to express those opinions.

Note

1   Carol Klein, *Cook Your Own Veg*, Mitchell Beazley, London (2008).

Re/drafting

On the grounds that very little writing is perfect first time, working with young writers on the process of reviewing and revising their work is important. This section focuses on some ways to embed drafting techniques in your students' everyday work.

There are three dominant positive outcomes that come from a well-taught approach to re/drafting writing. First, the process enables young writers to understand that a text that has been through a process of making incremental improvements will give the reader a better experience. This opportunity to develop the relationship between reader and writer is a step to children knowing that a text is nothing until it has a reader. Second, the process develops higher-order writing skills. Having been through repeated experiences of rewriting texts, students will adopt the improved model of how they write. In other words, each subsequent first draft will be closer to the improved version from last time's rewrite. This increases confidence and quality, which will be beneficial to outcomes in assessments. Third, the discourse around the rewriting process enriches classroom talk. It serves to develop a community of collaborative writers. With time the ideas in this section will become embedded and normalised, creating space for further development of skills and knowledge.

Think before you write. This seems obvious, but it is worth considering the importance of thinking before committing words to the page or screen. Thinking can take place silently in one's own head, can be spoken aloud with peers or can be scribbled on whiteboards. If we use the opening to a piece of spooky writing as an example, modelling a thought process could look something like this.

I want to get the reader to think about how cold and dark it is, so an opening sentence could be 'it was cold and dark in the quiet street' but that just tells the reader. To get them to use their imagination a bit more I'll change it to 'Adam pulled his hood up against the cold' which seems better, because now we know a character's name and I've shown the reader it's cold. Or, pulling his hood up could hint that he's hiding, so I still need to get the stuff about it being cold and dark. How about 'Adam shivered, pulled up his hood and tried to ignore the shadows cast by the street lights.' Now it seems like it's cold and dark and Adam seems a bit scared too, so it's a good start to a spooky story.

This thought process, getting a sentence ready in your head before writing it down works as pre-drafting, saving some work from later on, as your writers can have confidence that they got some of their text right, or close to right, first time.

Write then draft. This is the traditional model, and teachers are familiar with it, so to add something new you could experiment with automatic writing. Once you consider the class to be ready to write, set them going with the instruction that they need to write for a set period of time without stopping, correcting, revising or thinking in too much detail about anything. Writing in this way will mean that all students have some text with which they can work. At the end of the allotted time you can now start carving up the texts that have been produced. If you or another adult in the room have produced a piece of writing too, it can be used as the sample to teach next steps, some of which could be taken from the following list.

- Highlight words, phrases and sentences that are strong. This becomes the list of elements to keep.
- Underline words that need to be improved, whether it's the spelling or an alternative that is needed.
- Bracket off sentences that could be developed structurally, showing that there is some good content there but the way the reader receives it could be better.

Use peers as audience. In this model of drafting the writer gets to hear their own work read out, and in hearing it develops a sense of its efficacy. Working in this way demands that the room is set up for discussion, in pairs or groups of three. To begin, one student needs to read a completed text aloud and in full. It can be anyone in the group, it doesn't have to be the writer reading their own material. Once the group had heard the text in full, they need to go back to the start and read it again, this time with interruptions. Depending on the focus of the lesson, students may need to be guided to restrict their feedback to sentence structure, vocabulary, descriptive prowess, whatever you know is appropriate. The group will need to support the writer with praise too, and by making annotations so that the next version of the writing is genuinely based on what is captured in the discussions.

Finally, using a feedback sheet can be another approach to rewriting a text that ensures the writer gets quality input from a peer, or is guided through being critical of their own work. A resource bank of questions will facilitate this approach and could be used as an A5 handout. To build in appropriate levels of differentiation, the feedback sheet should cover technical and stylistic features of writing and you can use this list as a starting point for creating the resource.

- Was the writing planned?
- Are sentences accurate, with capital letters and full-stops?
- Are common words spelt correctly?
- Are there any spellings that need to be corrected?
- Does the writing fulfil its intended purpose?

- Will the intended audience find the text engaging?
- What are the highlights/best bits?

Once these questions have been addressed and returned to the original writer, collaborative efforts will have made sure that the next version of the text is improved and is on the way to fulfilling the relationship between the reader and writer.

Patterns and exceptions

The English language throws up all sorts of exceptions to the patterns that it follows. In spotting the exceptions we can firm up our understanding of the rule.

Apostrophes

Take for example the missing apostrophe from the possessive form of *its*. There should be an apostrophe if the word were to follow the rule. Your students could examine/explore why the rule is not followed in this example of an exception. On this occasion the exception is logical. There is a clash with the omission form of *it's*.

It is shortened to *it's* takes an apostrophe to show the omission of the letter *i*. If the possessive *its* were to follow the rule of adding an apostrophe then the two would be the same and indistinguishable. Therefore, the possessive *its* does not take the apostrophe. Rather than tell your students that this is the case, ask them to work it out when you are considering the use of apostrophes.

The simplest way to think this through is to have students say out loud the long form of 'it is' in the sentence that they are hoping to write and see if it is possible to say 'it is' and retain the sense. If you can say 'it is' then you need the apostrophe, if you can't then you don't. For example:

'Its/it's a sunny day.' You can say 'it is' here so an apostrophe is required.
'The cat ate its/it's dinner.' The cat ate *it is* dinner. No, so you don't have the apostrophe.

Plurals

A plural is generally made by adding an -*s* to the end of a word. This is the pattern that a baby learning English will discern and put into practice.

Sometimes, in writing, rather than adding -*s*, you add -*es*. If a word ends in *ch* or *sh* or *ss* or *x* then we apply an -*es*. Whilst being an exception to the rule of adding an -*s*, this is a further pattern in English.

Due to the nature of the English language there are more exceptions:

- on some words we add a different ending; examples would include words like oxen, crises and algae;
- sometimes we don't add any ending at all, e.g. sheep or cod;
- changing the vowel is another way to create plurals, e.g. man – men, mouse – mice;
- changing a consonant is also an option, e.g. wife – wives, leaf – leaves.
- sometimes in a compound it is the first element rather than the ending that can change, e.g. passer(s)-by.

Interestingly, sometimes there is more than one way to show a plural:

- cactus has two plural forms – cactuses and cacti;
- formula has formulas and formulae.

Even here, there is a regular pattern within the exception being made to the 'add an -s' rule. Each of these pairings has a more formal choice. Cacti and formulae are the more formal choice.

Ten tips for spellings

Getting your students to approach accurate spelling with a sense of hope and determination is a tough one. Kids tend to have made up their minds as to whether they can spell or not; those that are telling themselves that they can't, need to be encouraged out of this belief. Pointing out a few things to your students that demonstrate their abilities would be a good starting point.

1

Look at a page in their exercise books and underline any misspelt words. Select a page where there are just a couple. Then point out the fact that all the rest are right; 197 out of 200 isn't bad. Turn around the negative perspective to a more positive one. Even if only half the words are spelt right, this can be viewed in a more positive light. They are after all, half way there.

2

When students have completed a first paragraph of writing you could ask them to highlight all the words that they are confident are correct. This activity will help you measure the level of confidence that a student has in their ability to spell. It will also show you where they lack confidence. Look at the types and patterns of words that they are not sure about. In those words that they think are correct there may be some inaccurate spellings. This information will also support you in knowing where their competences lie.

3

Try an 'organic' spelling test. What we mean by this is a spelling test that includes words from the misspellings in their exercise books. Be clear that these are repeated patterns of misspelling and that just because it is one student's book does not mean that they are alone. In this way you are concentrating upon the words that they are actually using in their writing. The immediate, everyday active vocabulary that students are making use of is an important focus. This kind of test can seem very purposeful to students because it is addressing their actual needs.

4

Let's have a positive spelling test now and again. Ask the students to choose the longest words that they can spell. They select the words in an attempt to show their skill. Or start from a one letter word, then two letters, three and so on. They choose the words and keep going until they spell one wrong. It is a challenge and it can be fun.

5

Making use of the idea of collecting signs, get your students to bring in examples of misspellings that they see in their daily lives outside of school. In doing this they will actively be engaged in noticing. This is a good habit to get them into. It has so many benefits; increased curiosity around learning, making a link with the outside world and increasing ownership of learning being important amongst them.

6

Give every student a word of their own. All the words given out are 'hard to know' words. You explain that they are difficult words to spell. The students are to become the experts on their own individual words. They have to come up with good ways to remember how to spell the word. Each student presents their word to the class and the words are added to the display of these 'hard to know' words. The students will soon be boasting that even though these words are 'hard to know', well, not for them.

7

Students choose words that they find interesting/ones that they are struggling to spell. Get your students to search the internet, looking for their words in action. They have to find examples of the ways that writers are using those words. In this activity the students are examining the function of the word, perhaps getting a little closer to it in terms of meaning as well as seeing it spelt right over and over again.

8

When the going gets tough try scaffolding the spellings for students to try. By this we mean give every other letter and let your student fill in the gaps. For example:

i-m-d-a-e-y

This could become the format for a written spelling test or you might use it verbally as you go round the room.

'Tom. Look at that word again. It's not spelt quite right. Let's do it together. I'll
go first, i'
'm'
'm'
'e'

And so on. You build the word together and iron out the area of the word where the
misspelling is. In this way your student gets to think through their error rather than
you just correcting it. If you just correct it, it is more likely that the error will continue
to be made.

9

Other people's mistakes are always more palatable than your own. Students could
consider common mistakes that 'people' make. Look at the apostrophe rules in this
way. Students could be encouraged to discuss why 'people' often put the apostrophe in
'wasn't' in the wrong place, i.e. 'was'nt'. Students could be asked to discuss why
'people' often incorrectly move the *e* into the suffix *–ly*, for example, 'immediatley',
'accuratley' and 'fortunatley'. Again, this is helpful as the emphasis is on exploring and
understanding errors, and in doing this, developing strategies for being thoughtful and
accurate around approaching spelling more generally.

10

There is a great deal of angst at the moment about students being right first time, every
time. We think that it comes from an anxiety around students having to pass their
exams and tests. Given that we are all fallible when it comes to spelling, and no one can
be expected to spell all words correctly, we think we need to embrace the making of
mistakes a bit more. Your classroom needs to be a place where it is okay to spell words
incorrectly, a place where there are strategies for thinking about these errors. Perhaps
the students could find the hardest words they can and then they could test you. Show
them that it is okay to be wrong as long as you think through how you will get the
spelling right another day.

Big, deep and wide questions

Questioning in the classroom has come under a good deal of scrutiny in recent years. The model of the teacher asking a question with a definite answer, choosing a respondent in under a second and then praising the answer before moving on to a separate question has its limitations. As much as anything else, asking people questions that they know the answer to in under a second doesn't seem to move them on very much. Better, we think, to ask questions that students can't immediately answer, or to which they don't yet have an answer, or, even better still, they may never have a full answer to.

The value of talk in the classroom is increasingly recognised. Speaking activates a different kind of memory to writing. Talk can often act as a vehicle for writing. When students speak they get to say what they think, they get to take ownership of the learning. In listening to others they can measure what they think against the views of the speaker. They can refine their thinking, shape their ideas.

Here is an example of a question that requires some active thinking through.

If speaking and writing were to have a race, which one would win?

This is great fun, but not immediately answerable. Students may well get in to a debate about what the race might be. Perhaps the 'race' is to communicate as quickly and effectively as possible. They might take into account the mode of paper and pen and screen and keyboard against speech and the mobile phone. Whilst they are discussing this, your students are yet again sifting language; looking at its properties and its potential.

Here is another example.

Who has to think more, the person that writes a letter or the person that reads it?

Again, this question will have your students thinking through the properties of language. Teaching to tests seems to mean generally that we help students make sense of things through simplifying those things for them. We are not sure that that is a productive way forward. Better still to make sense for students through enquiry and relevance. These questions create the opportunity to explore the purpose and systems of language, searching for how language functions in the 'real world'.

Think up questions like this for yourself. The power of this type of thinking is not to be under-estimated. Students need to be encouraged to think about questions that demand their perseverance, that require them to explore past what they know and to be prepared to not have a fully formed answer ready. This sort of work makes the brain more 'muscular', increases the connections between the parts of the brain and makes your students more self-reliant as learners.

Why is it that you can tune a piano but you can't tuna fish?

Oh, hang on. That one's just silly.

Making up new words

Here's some fun with language. Get your students to make up a new word. This begs the question, when is a word a word, and when is a word a wannabe word? Your group could discuss this aspect of the task. How will they know when their word has made it into the English language? This will probably elicit a response around the idea that a word is officially a word when it appears in the dictionary. So, how does a word get included in the dictionary? And there you have another investigation ready to happen for the group.

It would be good to look at the Oxford English Dictionary to see how words are collected there. It would also be good to check out the Urban Dictionary and the way that words make it into that particular type of dictionary. Be warned: much of the content of the Urban Dictionary is inappropriate. You will need to extract definitions for studying with your students.

In essence, a word gets to be a word if a group of speakers – friends, family, and speakers of a language – agree that it has a certain meaning and then they make use of that word. The word is understood and it has a function. The dictionary includes ways in which the word is used.

You invite your students to think up a new word. Ours is *blabbed*. Our new word will be the word for the feeling you get when you have eaten so much that you are completely full. Our example of its use is as follows:

'That was great but I'm blabbed. I couldn't eat another thing.'

Your students make definitions for their words and they give examples of their words in action. Could you put the students into groups to create little role plays in which each of their new words are used? Perhaps the audience have to define the words from the ways they are being used in the role play.

You could discuss what would need to happen for your new words to make it past the confines of the classroom. How would these new words make it into the real world? This might take you into discussion about the power of the media. You could explore where new words and phrases have come from recently. This might lead you into looking at how most of the time new words and expressions are made by using already existing words, as in the example 'credit crunch'. You might get your students to make up new expressions based on this compounding. Even more fun is to get them to make up some blends. This is where two existing words have been blended together to make one new word, usually using the beginning of one word and the end of the other, as in the example motor – hotel = motel, or the more recent restaurant – entertainment = restaurantainment.

Being creative is a high order skill. Making up new words and thinking through the factors that might be involved really gets your students thinking carefully about their language.

Difficult words/punctuation

There are no uncurious children. They just don't exist. Kids all want to know stuff. It might not always be the stuff you want them to learn, but they all want to know stuff. The oft-heard teacher expression, 'He just isn't interested' just doesn't ring true. Wherever possible with students that are 'uninterested' the trick is to look to the real world around them. Get them investigating things. Get their heads up, get them looking around themselves. Make your curriculum needs fit the kid and the environment. This supports making the learning relevant. Once it has that relevance then the interest can spark long-term memory – and that is where you want your learning to be.

Some words, some expressions are just difficult. Some punctuation is hard to get right. Everyone has problem words and phrases that they need to sort out.

You and your students could set out to help people get their spellings and their grammar up to scratch. Send your students off round the school to interview people to find out what the problems are. Perhaps one visit could be paid to the cook, one to the headteacher, one to the caretaker and one to the nurse, etc.

Your students collect the 'problems'. They could also take a photo of the person – for display purposes – and promise to get back to them with some help and guidance. Back in class, round up the problems and groups of experts are assigned to different problems. They explore ways of dealing with the issues and prepare some helpful advice. The advice could be made into posters that are then displayed around school. The picture of the member of staff is accompanied with a short statement of their problem and then the advice is displayed below.

This activity has a number of audiences and adds cumulatively to the general awareness of writing in the school at large. First, we have the investigator them self. He/she is sifting language, looking at a common problem and reflecting upon how to solve it. The sense of expert is given to them. They are empowered as they are fixing other people's problems rather than fretting about their own. The burden of being wrong is shared and, we think, given a sense of proportion. It is okay not to be able to do everything easily. The adult members of staff have shared this insight by sharing their own little technical issues with writing.

Second, and importantly, the school is full of posters by the kids that indicate that learning the technical side of writing is manageable. The ethos of the school to writing is good. There are practical tips that a student can pick up on the corridor.

And, of course, hopefully, your students can support the learning of the adults in the school.

This activity could, of course, also be done at home. Students find out about the words, phrases and punctuation that their families struggle with. Again, the connection with the real world makes the abstract world of grammar learning a bit more relevant.

Cut and paste fun

You want your students to do some creative and independent writing. This is exactly as it should be. When they reach their adult lives they won't have people standing over them, advising them on the qualities of their writing. They need the chance to write independently at school before this support mechanism – you – is withdrawn.

But there are always those students who, when faced with the impossibility of the blank page, just can't get going – 'I don't know what to write, Miss' – as if there is some 'right' content/formula that they are failing to live up to. Children can find this situation difficult and frustrating. This situation is exacerbated these days by the fact that students hardly ever use paper and pen, as you are asking them to do with this creative writing.

Perhaps the digital native needs a digital environment. Here's an idea: students are to work on the computer today. Ah, things are already feeling more like home. Instead of an empty page you offer the students a page full of text. The actual text doesn't really matter, just so long as there is plenty of it. The students are then set the task of cutting and pasting. They are to write a fresh piece of writing but making use of the text on the screen. They can delete words, create new sentences and change the punctuation. They are able to introduce new words as well. The full page stops the fear of the empty page and there are no children who resent cutting and pasting on a computer like they might do when filling the blank page with a pen.

As your students set about the task, they are exploring the usefulness of words. They are searching for a story in a sea of language. The possible employment of vocabulary and the reshaping of sentences are all aspects of the task. They are genuinely multi-tasking. All the contributing skills of writing are coming together at the same time as they pursue their creative writing.

To our mind, this is the natural place for thinking about grammar, embedded in the craft of writing. It is so much more useful than the learning of grammatical features in isolation. Here we are looking at the employment of structure and phrase in a real setting – that of actually writing for a purpose.

Evidently, this process can be extended to all types of writing. A page from a novel could be turned into a poem. The student is asked, in writing the poem, to reflect upon the nature of the character that was being discussed on the page of the novel. All you have done is remove the blank page and the stumbling block to getting going; with text to work with you have pitched the writer into the middle of the writing with many jobs ahead to make a new piece of writing. We promise you that the natural instinct that we all have to organise language will kick in.

Dramatic readings

Your students need to be directed to the functions of the grammatical features of the texts that you want them to engage with. In supporting them to think about the way a writer has employed sentence structures and punctuation, your students will become better at employing these features themselves but they will also become stronger readers and interpreters of texts.

Whilst you are working on a class reader perhaps you could ask your students to plan and deliver a dramatic reading of a passage from the text. Whether they work individually, in pairs or in groups would very much depend on your judgement of the needs of the children in front of you. However they are organised, ask them to make annotations on the extract that you have chosen. Perhaps you could tell them that they are going to do the reading for an audio book version of the story. You and your group could discuss how a reader of an audio book needs to speak if the story is to be as successful as possible. Maybe a reading could be chosen to go on the website or to be used with other groups in the year.

What will the students have to make annotations for? We think that we would begin by asking them. How do you make a dramatic reading? Hopefully they will talk about the need for emphasis on certain words, the potential of getting louder and quieter, the use of pauses for effect, etc. Maybe they will think about a system to indicate the various features of the way they want to deliver the reading. Underlining might mean emphasis. If you are using technology, emboldening text might serve the same function. Brackets might be used to house instructions to the reader to go quieter or louder. A set of brackets with a dot in might be the signal to take a particular pause.

This is yet another example of an activity where the text is already there and you are asking your students to manipulate it rather than generating a whole new text. This is not dumbing down. The fact that the student doesn't write a text on this occasion is just because that writing is not the intended outcome this time. You want to focus on the construction of writing. Whilst your students are making choices about where to pause, where to speed up, where to alter their voices to show emotion, they are actively considering the make-up of writing through its structural devices. This is encouraging procedural knowledge. They are sifting the text trying to develop its meaning through a spoken presentation of that meaning.

What you make of the fruits of this labour is open to all sorts of outcomes. You might have a speaking competition, use the spoken extracts with another group in their reading of the text or get the students to add a PowerPoint display of images to go with the reading. Each and any of these ideas increase the sense that this is a 'real' and purposeful thing to be doing in the classroom.

The grammar of photography

In investigating the grammatical structures of writing, do you think that there is any merit in looking at the structures of other forms of art? Let's look at the example that we offer here, photography. What are the grammatical features of a photograph? We are sure that your students will be able to play around with this idea.

The following example refers to a photograph, *Migrant Mother*, by Dorothea Lange, which makes a really good example. You, of course, can very well choose photographs of your own!

Photographs have edges. You can't see either side, above or below. This, if you excuse the pun, frames the image. In this photograph it is hard to see where the people are and that makes demands on the imagination of the viewer. The person looking at the picture has to fill in their own context based on clues/guesses from what they can see.

The photograph is in black and white. Was this for effect or does the photo come from a time before colour film was available? If it is intentionally black and white, what impact does this have on the image?

Where is the focal point of the photo? Where are the eyes drawn to? How do the different lines in the image move the eye of the viewer about? The face of the baby resting on the woman's lap – in the bottom right hand corner – can be difficult to see at first. What is the impact of 'finding' it?

Who do we think is taking the photograph? Why are they taking the photograph?

If you pose the question, 'What is this photograph about?' rather than, 'What can you see in the photograph?' you will get a much broader set of answers. Your students might very well decide that this is a very poor mother with her children and that the mother is thinking about where on earth she is going to get the next meal to feed the children with. Ask your students how the photograph has brought them to this conclusion. The colour, the edges, the lines, etc. are the grammar of the photograph.

This photograph could then lead you very nicely into a writing activity. The students have told you that the photograph does not allow the viewer to know the context of the story behind these people's lives. Can your students now write a descriptive piece that does the same? They describe the poverty of the people without giving the background or 'story'. What will be the focal point of the writing? Will it be the searching eyes of the mother? What sort of sentences will best give a sense of the woman's distress? What vocabulary will best express her troubles?

Having thought about the grammar of photography, you could extend this activity to getting your students to take photographs that tell a story and then get them to think through the grammar/the structure of their photographs. The opportunity for a vibrant and colourful display around the grammar of photography is just too good to resist.

If you were to use this Dorothea Lange photograph *Migrant Mother* from 1936, there is a whole raft of information about the photographer, loads of related photographs and the plight of the migrant workers of the dustbowl years in America. Happily, you can also see photographs of the woman in the photograph, Florence Owens Thompson, as an old lady, surrounded by her family. Your students will be pleased with the happy ending.

Clearly this approach of searching for the grammar in other forms of art is applicable across a whole range. Paintings will do just as well as photographs. Students would obviously enjoy looking at the structure of pop music as well. If you are not careful, this grammar thing could be a lot of fun.

Innate competence

There is a temptation in teaching to treat the students as blank canvasses, or vessels that need filling with your education. You are the teacher and you know things, and these things you know have to be known by the students. It is an easy starting point to make, especially with the exams hanging over all of you! If you start from here with grammar then you are missing a trick. The kids know stuff and they don't even know it! The trick is to tap in to that innate ability.

When babies learn to speak they do it because it is an instinctive drive within them. They want to join in, they want to be human. They learn at the age of about one that the pleasurable noises that they can make with their mouths and lips have meaning and purpose, and structure. They have been practising the patterns and sound of their own language and become ready to join in. As their capacities increase, children are able to say single words and begin to express themselves.

Once a child puts one word next to another we have the sophisticated leap towards human speech. A two-word utterance is a grammatical construction. Each word has an impact upon the other. The meaning of the word *road* is altered when it is put next to the word *closed*. In fact the meaning of both words is adapted. Nobody teaches a child the skill of putting two words together to make a new set of meaning. They listen to the sounds around them, they store those sounds as responses to contexts and they develop the ability to sift through those sounds/words to make new constructions that they have never heard spoken out loud before.

As their language develops further, children learn how to make the past tense by adding -*ed*. When a baby says, 'we wented' it is an error but a very clever one. The child has learnt the rule about making the past tense and is applying it consistently. On occasion, with a language packed with irregularities, an error will crop up. But this error demonstrates the innate ability of the child to organise language. It is the same with making plurals by adding –*s*: 'I see sheeps' makes the same point as 'wented'.

By the time a child is three they are able to express themselves with a good deal of clarity. By the time they are six their grammatical understanding is fixed, locked in to the structures and systems of their mother tongue. This is one of the reasons that learning the grammar of a foreign language can be so difficult. Your brain has already settled on the grammatical structures that allow you to speak, and by extension, to write.

Can we make use of this 'knowledge' of language and its application in our students to get them to explore how language works? Here is a fun activity that you could try with your students. Tell them that they have two minutes to work out/translate the writing that you are going to put on the whiteboard. Here is the text:

> Quando si fermarono lui fece altrettanto, abbastanza vicino per sentire quel che dicevano.
> 'Allora, binario numero?' chiese la donna, che era la madre dei ragazzi.

Now that is going to be really hard/impossible without a few Italians in the room! It can be a good deal of fun though listening to the brave coming up with answers. So, admit that that wasn't fair and say that you are going to show them the text again but this time you are going to give them the translation. Here is the translation:

> They stopped and so did he, just near enough to hear what they were saying.
> 'Now, what's the platform number?' said the boy's mother.

Change the question. Now you want to know what they can tell about the Italian language from the translation. Having scaffolded the activity in this way, you should (we have done this loads of times and it always works for us!) get a good number of observations about Italian.

Some might say that the language is more beautiful than English. Some will think that it has longer words. Some will notice that lots of words end in a vowel. Some will see that the grammatical structures might be different. Some will think that it might have a gender case system like in French. What the students are doing is measuring and sifting the Italian, making comparison with English and, like my example of French, with languages more broadly.

You can say to your students, 'Look at this. We have been learning Italian for four minutes and you have been able to tell me all these things about the way Italian is … and, I haven't taught you anything. I haven't told you anything about it. You knew it already.'

And it is true. What you have done is to make use of their innate understanding of how languages are.

Here is another example activity. Show your students the first line of the poem 'This is just to say' by William Carlos Williams (1883–1963)[1]:

> I have eaten

Now ask them to write the next line. Invariably they will write a short line with two or three words. This is because their understanding of language tells them that this is likely to be the case. The first line was short so the second will also be short. What they write will also make sense when read with the first. Again, this is because your students understand how language works. They will try to build on the sense of the first line.

You can repeat this activity line by line. The poem has three short verses of four lines each. When you reveal line five and there is nothing on it as it is the gap between verse one and verse two you can be sure that most will estimate that there will be a line break on line ten as well. They are applying the structures and forms of language that they have developed instinctively.

Note

1   William Carlos Williams, available at www.poetryfoundation.org/poem/245576

Playing with word class

Sometimes what seems to be the most straightforward can be the most complex. If you asked your students, or colleagues, if they know what a word is chances are you'd get a very high rate of positive responses. If you asked them to define what a word is, it's likely that things would get a little more tricky. This is very much a problem for linguists, too.

The reason for this is because a word is a function rather than a fixed thing. Unlike a full stop or a comma, which are always consistent in both form and function, words are slippery and mean different things in different contexts. Let's take the fairly innocuous word, *fine*, and see how it operates in different contexts. We can talk about fine art (*fine* as an adjective to demonstrate quality), fine hair (*fine* as an adjective to demonstrate thinness), a parking *fine* (fine as a noun), if a law is broken an individual may be fined (*fine* as a verb) or when asked how things are we might respond, 'fine' (*fine* as an adverb).

So *fine* is at least five different words and serves as at least four different word classes. It even has meanings that are at odds with one another. There is a huge difference between the high social status and expense because certain artworks are considered 'fine' when compared to the adverbial form which is at best a non-committal way of saying things are ok, average, could be better and could be worse.

The focus of this section is developing an understanding of the ways that words can function differently, therefore developing an understanding that language and meanings are context bound.

You can start by leading a class discussion about words that can belong to more than one word class. You could pick one from this list to demonstrate the topic.

light	shop	plant	rain
play	water	word	study
wind	place	act	credit
hand			

By demonstrating how any word from this list can work in different ways you can then open up the discussion about how meanings come from the context in which a word is placed rather than a word having a fixed meaning. As worthwhile consolidation, the children could write a few sentences to demonstrate that they get it, like the examples below using 'hand'.

> My hand is at the end of my arm. (noun)
> Would you hand me the ropes? (verb)
> Can I use your hand cream please? (adjective)

Writing these sentences shows that we understand some of the ways that words can be used in a variety of contexts. In the first example it is possible to work out that because the sentence begins with the possessive determiner 'my' we know that something that belongs to the speaker is going to be mentioned. In the second example 'hand' serves as a verb because it is the act between two or more people. We can test this further by replacing it with other verbs, such as 'pass' or 'give'. In the final example 'hand' is the pre-modifier that shows precisely which cream is being requested. In this adjectival form it describes the cream and creates clarity.

Moving past this identification and analysis of word classes and with some secure understanding in place, it's time to get creative. In his poem 'Pike'[1] Ted Hughes describes the fish as:

> Pike, three inches long, perfect
> Pike in all parts, green tigering the gold.
> Killers from the egg: the malevolent aged grin.
> They dance on the surface among the flies.

Hughes has redefined the noun, *tiger*, as a verb. We know because of the position of the word in the sentence, and because the *-ing* ending is the grammatical feature that creates a verb in the progressive form. To make this point to your class it will be helpful to pull up an image of a pike, especially a live fish with good enough lighting in the photograph to show the colouring on its sides. Ask the students to consider how they understand Hughes' use of 'tigering'. They can't look it up in a dictionary because the verb isn't acknowledged as a word. It's only through looking at pictures of pike, reading the verse of the poem and applying an understanding of tigers can a meaning be created.

This creates a very personal sense of meaning between the reader and the text. Working with your student writers to create this intimate sense of meaning can be a powerful way to show that language belongs to them. It isn't a topic for study and testing, it's as much a part of them as their intestines or their thoughts.

Descriptive writing lends itself to this way of playing with language as that is where readers expect to be challenged to think and recreate the images the writer created. It's also inappropriate in more formal writing. Animals are a useful place to start. We already have examples in everyday language. *Ferreting, rabbiting, worming* and *hawking* are commonplace words and you can start people off by showing a series of images of, perhaps, a camel, a lion, a lizard and a mole. Turning these nouns into progressive verbs and then thinking of how they might be used in descriptions gives the students the chance to be playful with their language.

Note

1   Ted Hughes, *New and Selected Poems*, Faber, London (2010).

Explicit modelling of writing

It is hard to overestimate how influential a teacher can be in the learning of a student. However your students view their own abilities as learners, they understand that you are the expert. You are an authority (whether you know your stuff or not!). Your word is the accepted law on all matters. Whilst the activities suggested here are often about students investigating for themselves, there are times when you can make use of your elevated status.

You can model the process of writing. Armed with strong information from formative assessment (see, for example, the section on marginal commentaries earlier) you can select the type of instruction that might usefully be made in an explicit manner.

Let's take the example of openings to stories. Students often find the blank page and a freedom associated with creative writing leaves them with writer's block. They just don't know how to begin. As you create the opening to your story you speak your thoughts, making it clear what thinking is going into the creation of the writing. Let's call it writing out loud.

For example:

> 'I want to write an opening to my story that holds back some information from the reader so that they are immediately made curious about what is going on. I am going to use the first person but I am not going to let the reader know who the speaker is just yet. Let's see – "My problem began the day the river burst its banks." Or perhaps "my problems". That's better, more than one problem. Adds to the idea that the person speaking has a lot to sort out. Yes, this sentence opens up lots of interest. Why has the river burst its banks? Is there a connection between the river bursting its banks and the problems? That would seem to make sense as they are in the same sentence. The connection is implied. Would it be better if it were the night that the river burst its banks? Does the idea of it being at night add to the drama? The sentence is a simple one. I think that makes it quite a striking opening. Okay, where to next ... '

This commentary around the thinking that a writer might go through can encourage a similarly analytical approach in your students. Thinking through the actual choice of words for a story is often neglected by young writers because they get absorbed in plot development. The choice of words can often be the first ones that come to mind. Pointing out that a writer hopes to make an impact on a reader opens up the thought that the choices of words will have a strong impact on whether a story is engaging or not.

By extension, you could ask your students to 'write aloud' with each other. The practice of speaking through your decision-making as you work has much broader applications to offer. Playing with grammar and selecting vocabulary for impact is surely the point of studying the technical side of writing at school. We are in the business of making communicators. This kind of explicit out-loud thinking is a useful way of getting students to be thoughtful about language choices.

Ask the author

What we offer students in the classroom needs to be relevant to their lives. If a student were to ask you what the point of the lesson is and you can't answer, then perhaps you should stop the lesson!

One way to be sure of relevance in writing is to have a sense of real audiences and real purposes to the writing that you ask students to produce. Handing writing to you for your approval/correction is quite limited in terms of audience. Indeed, it might feel like no audience at all – merely part of the obligation of going to school; you do work and it is marked.

A text involves someone that has written the text and someone who is going to read the text. The writer will have intentions and purposes around what they have written and the reader will make their own meaning from the text in front of them. Helping students understand that writers and readers don't always see the text in the same way is an important step towards getting students to understand that the way they write something is equally important as the content itself. The quality of expression will carry much of the impact.

Can you find audiences for your writers?

Are there other classes in school that might read and comment on your students' work? Are there local schools that you could team up with to share writing projects? Can you identify audiences that require something to read before you start the writing? Can you take an approach in which there is a 'client' audience for whom your students will write? Do you have the means to publish the writing of your students beyond the walls of your own classroom? Will your headteacher pay to have a vanity book published? Can you contribute performances of writing to an arts evening at school? Can you support your students in setting up blogsites?

Can you put readers in touch with writers?

Many authors are much more easily accessible in these days of Twitter and Facebook accounts. A good number are very happy to respond to enquiries about their work. Articles in newspapers list not only the name of the journalist that wrote the article but often their email address as well. Again, a good number are happy to respond about the things that they have written. The students, of course, have each other. They can question each other about the writing that they have done. This sort of enquiry sharpens the act of writing through reflection upon what has been achieved.

As a starting point, can your students suggest the texts that they would like to write? What are the burning issues and subjects that they would like to write about? Is there any genuine reason to deny them the opportunity to make selections of topics and formats? That sense of ownership will surely improve motivation around writing. The sense that the student has selected the writing increases impetus.

Flexing your vocabulary brain

Here are some quick word exercises that will help get brains active in the classroom. They could be but don't have to be starters. They could be, but don't have to be, used at transition points in a lesson. They could be group work or they could be an activity that the whole class does together.

* Write the longest sentence string that you can using words that have the same number of letters. Try out different numbers of letters, e.g.:

  When free, call this line that will give some help with ... etc.

* Write a sentence string in which the words have increasingly greater numbers of letters, e.g.:

  I am not here every Monday because ... etc.

* Write a list of words that include all the vowels, e.g.: unrecognisable.
* Take a four-letter word and change one letter after another (at each change there is still a recognisable word) until you have a second word that you have asked for., e.g.: hard – soft. Try to complete the chain in as few moves as possible:

  HARD – lard – lord – cord – card – cart – tart – part – port – sort – SOFT

* Offer the students three-letter combinations and ask them to write down as many words as they can with those letters appearing together, e.g.: 'ght', 'iou' or 'ely'. In this way you can explore patterns of spelling that students find difficult. Double consonants and vowel sounds would be common ones that you might want to pursue.
* Can your students find/think of words that have all of their letters appearing in alphabetical order? For example: *first*. What is the longest word they can come up with?
* Try to make word strings in which the last two letters of one word become the first two of the next. How long can you make the string? Each word should have the same number of letters. This is not as easy as it may sound. For example: river – erase – serve – verve – vexed – ed? You can soon get stuck. Perhaps have this activity running on a timer.

- Offer nine random letters. Students need to make as many words as they can using, let's say, five of the letters each time to create new words. Change the number of letters, put the timer on, mix it up.

  r – n – m – e – a – h – s – I – d
  meals, deals, names

  Change the activity to using as many of the letters as possible in a new word.

  REHeArSaL (score: 6)

You can think of many, many more of these kinds of games and puzzles. They get the brain up and running. Used at transition points they can switch the brain back on to being alert. If you can incorporate some physical movement into the activities as well that also will increase alertness when the students sit back down. Your students will enjoy the non-threatening levels of challenge here and if it becomes a classroom norm, they will come to expect challenge in your room.

   Try these activities out. Different sets of students will enjoy different ones. Make some more up of your own.

Redundancy in language

Grammar needs authority if it is to work. Rules are taught about spelling and grammatical patterns. This can have the side effect of students accepting grammar just because 'it is the rules'. Some thought into the way that the system of grammatical structure works would be good in widening your students' sense of the necessity and purposefulness of grammar.

Scientists, creationists, philosophers and the like have spent a lot of time considering whether the world is systematic or chaotic. Mathematicians, physicists and economists look for system within chaotic structures. Much has been made of the butterfly effect setting off chains of events; whether these chains are random or predetermined is the subject of much debate.

We could look carefully at the make-up of language as a part of this debate. What is systematic and what is random about our capacity to talk in sounds, and to represent those sounds in written form? An interesting place for your students to start here is the fact that not every sound or pattern is purposeful and this is a very important factor if language is to work successfully. Words and grammatical structures need space in which to exist and there has to be an element of redundancy within the language. Some sounds must mean nothing. But why is this so? Here are a number of ways of unpacking the idea that language has built in redundancy.

When is a word a word?

Let us look at the word ending -*ind*. This combination of letters can be used in a number of four letter words; *bind, find, hind, kind, mind, rind, wind*. So why can't the rest of the letters start words with that ending; *sind, nind, yind, zind* – all look okay, but they are not words with recognised meanings. What would be the outcome for speakers of the language if every combination of every series of letters had meaning? Notice also that *ind* itself, whilst making up part of a word, is not a word in itself. What is gained by some combinations of sounds and letters not having any recognisable meanings? There is space for the sounds to which we have ascribed meaning to move around in. There is potential for new words to be formed; either through compounding or blending existing meaningful shapes or in creating neologisms.

Searching for meaning

There are 44 sounds used in the English language but they are not all used in every combination. The language has built-in redundancy. If every sound were productive, comprehension would be hindered. As you speak, the words largely run together and the listener needs to be able to make sense of the sounds that you are making. Words are only identifiable if some sounds are not words.

Iwasonlysayingtheotherdaythatthepriceofpeaskeepsgoingup

As you look at the sentence above you are instinctively pulling the units of meaning apart from each other. You are searching for the meaning within a structure that has redundant features. The whole string of letters does not mean anything in itself. Neither do random portions of it, for example 'erdayt' or 'epsgo'. Meaning is packaged in the meaningless.

A systematic language?

Let's try to make a very systematic language. Let's ascribe sound patterns to words that are related by subject matter. We shall use *ubshat* to mean stationery and we will use different endings to represent the related items. Here we go:

ubshat	stationery
ubshata	pencil
ubshate	ruler
ubshati	sharpener
ubshatum	rubber

And so on and so on. Your students could consider whether this highly organised and structured vocabulary is helpful or not. We think that it might make a visit to the stationers a bit difficult. The beauty of the difference of pencil, rubber, sharpener and ruler is that they are all immediately distinguishable from each other. The *ubshat* collection of words lacks that immediate difference in sound that supports meaning. Chinese whispers comes to mind.

Redundancy in grammar

Grammar	phonology	discourse
Semantics	lexis	*language*

This is a word picture. Does it have any meaning? The words are randomly placed around the page. Can links be made between the words? Certainly they share a common theme. What does this say about the structure of grammar? The structure of language is so redundant that we are still able to make sense of the text without any recognisable grammatical structures in place to organise the text. You could get your students to create sets of five words that reveal a sixth that the rest of the students guess at.

Foreign languages as a clue to redundancy

When we study foreign languages at school there is a good deal of vocabulary to be learned. In French, for instance, we learn that the word for *apple* is *pomme*. My computer has just underlined the word *pomme* because it is not a word. Instead I have been offered *pommel* or *pummel* as options. What do we mean by the expression, 'The word for apple is pomme'? The very idea that similar senses in languages are carried by different patterns of letters and sounds indicates further the element of redundancy within language. Our perspective is shaped by our own context.

We think that the idea of redundancy can be an important and fun way in for your students' understanding of how language, and grammar in particular, works. Hopefully, the approaches above will give you some accessible ways in.

Glossary

A glossary of terms

The following glossary is for your use in growing confidence around the technical language of grammar. The list covers the requirements of Key Stage 2 and 3 curricular documents and is certainly more than comprehensive as a checklist in preparing for tests across those Key Stages. More importantly, it offers good coverage in preparing writers to be writers who can make informed choices about how they write.

We have spoken in many schools about grammar and there is often a frightened look on the faces of many of our teacher colleagues in the audience as they are faced with long lists of the terminology of grammar. You need to feel confident across a broad range of grammatical knowledge. Your confidence is not just about being able to fend off difficult questions from students! It is about informing the process of making valuable lesson ideas. Once you know the scope of grammatical knowledge and you feel secure in your understanding, we think that you will feel more resourceful. That confidence will breed resourcefulness, both in yourself/you (which is it?) and in your students.

These terms are certainly not for passing on to your students in this form. Passing on information to students has never been more difficult. The invention of the internet means that your students already have a vast reservoir of information in their pockets. They can choose what information they are interested enough to look at. You can direct them to 'child-friendly' material but this list of grammar terms is unlikely to be able to compete!

As a year-long project, recreating this glossary with your students would result in two things: first, the re-written glossary, definitions and examples created by students are more likely to be remembered; second, the very act of being able to compile a glossary demands a secure knowledge of the terms that it seeks to define.

Active – Passive
An active verb has a usual pattern of subject and object (in contrast with the passive).

Active:

> The agent arranged a visit. The travel company made a mistake. It is suggested that both were negligent.

Passive:

> A visit was arranged by the agent. A mistake was made by the travel company. There has been a suggestion of negligence on both their parts.

This can be an aspect of language that students find difficult to appreciate. Getting them to analyse texts that make use of the passive rather than the active can be useful when it comes to thinking about how to approach a particular audience or in getting over a particular argument. Students could look at how politicians sometimes use the passive to distant themselves from the bad news or blame that they are speaking about.

Adjectives

Adjectives can be explained to students as 'describing words' because they are used to pick out single characteristics such as size or colour.

It is sometimes hard to pick out adjectives from some other word classes. The best way to be able to identify adjectives is by looking at the ways they are used. This idea of identifying grammatical features through considering the ways in which they function has a wide number of applications.

- Before a noun, to make the noun's meaning more specific (i.e. to modify the noun).
- Example: Peter Beardsley made a really <u>good</u> pass to Alan Shearer.
- After the verb *be*, as its complement
- Example: His motivation was <u>excellent</u>.

Adjectives cannot be modified by other adjectives. This distinguishes them from nouns, which can be. This is often true, but it doesn't help to distinguish adjectives from other word classes. The following sentences demonstrate different word classes that might appear to be adjectives.

> The worm <u>glowed</u>. [in this instance the word *glowed* is a verb]
> He spoke <u>quietly</u>. [here we have an adverb. The word quietly is modifying a verb rather than a noun]

Adverbs

Adverbs are used to describe manner or time. In the SP&G test your students may well be asked to spot adverbs (useful, we know!)

The best way to identify adverbs is by looking at the ways they can be used: they can modify a verb, an adjective, another adverb or even a whole clause.

> Simon soon started crying loudly. [here the adverb is modifying the verbs *started* and *crying*]
> That programme was really exciting! [here the adverb is modifying the adjective *exciting*]

We don't get to play scrabble very often. [here the adverb is modifying the other adverb, *often*]

Fortunately, it didn't freeze. [here the adverb is modifying the whole clause 'it didn't freeze' by commenting on it]

Antonyms

Two words are antonyms if their meanings are opposites. Students will quite happily find these pairings for you, and there are plenty of them to be found.

    hot – cold
    light – dark
    light – heavy

Apostrophes

The apostrophe is one of the points of grammar that teachers spend the most time working on. No matter what you do, it seems that children find it a hard punctuation mark to get right. This is largely because the apostrophe doesn't make a sound; you don't 'hear it' in your head as you construct writing. To a certain extent, the apostrophe is losing its authority because very little is lost in terms of communication if it isn't there. *Isnt* without the apostrophe is still entirely clear and this is largely the case whenever an apostrophe is not there.

   Apostrophes have two completely different uses: first, showing the place of missing letters (e.g. *I'm* for *I am*). This is called omission.

   I'm going out and I won't be long. [showing missing letters]

Second, showing that something belongs to someone or something. This is called possession.

   Tim's brother went to Oakville in Peter's van.

There are a number of exceptions that don't take the apostrophe: *theirs, yours, ours, his, hers, its*. A particular problem in children's writing occurs around the exception made for the possessive form of its.

   It's – it is/its – the cat its dinner (the possessive doesn't take the apostrophe that it would if it were to follow the rule. This is to avoid confusion with the omission *it's*).

Articles

The articles *the* (definite) and *a* or *an* (indefinite) are the most common type of determiner.

   The dog found a bone in an old box.

The choice of article can make quite a difference in your students' writing. There is a good deal of difference in the impact created in the sentence, 'He opened the door' and 'He opened a door'. The indefinite article opens up interpretation whilst the definite article is more exact. Thinking through which to choose can focus students clearly on the careful construction of their writing.

Brackets

There are a number of different types of brackets and they are employed over a range of uses. They also have different names in different parts of the world.

- ( ) — parentheses, brackets (UK, Canada, New Zealand, and Australia), parens, round brackets, soft brackets, or circle brackets.
  The most commonly used brackets for the purpose of clarifying what is being said or to make a remark aside.
- [ ] — square brackets, closed brackets, hard brackets, or brackets (US).
  These brackets are generally used to add explanatory information or to indicate where there is a gap in the text, some text having been omitted.
- { } — braces (UK and US), flower brackets (India), French brackets, curly brackets, definite brackets, swirly brackets, curly braces, birdie brackets, Scottish brackets, squirrelly brackets, gullwings, seagulls, squiggly brackets, twirly brackets, Tuborg brackets (DK), accolades (NL), pointy brackets, or fancy brackets.
  Used in music, mathematics and in writing. In music the curly brackets are used to show lines of notes that are played together. In mathematics and writing, the brackets are used to show the limits of a set, for example {house cottage bungalow flat}
- < > — pointy brackets, angle brackets, triangular brackets, diamond brackets, tuples, or chevrons.
  Again, these brackets serve different functions in different disciplines. In writing they are used to indicate where an older text that is being referenced has lines that are illegible or otherwise lost.

There are a good number of other types of brackets. Perhaps your students might be set the task to investigate different types and t report back to the group.

Clauses, types of

A clause is a type of phrase whose focus is a verb.

Clauses can sometimes be complete sentences. Clauses may be main or subordinate.

Traditionally, a clause had to have a finite verb, but most modern grammarians also recognise non-finite clauses.

It was windy. [single-clause sentence]
It was sunny but we were indoors.[two finite clauses]
If you are coming to the concert, please let us know. [finite subordinate clause inside a finite main clause]

Amy went upstairs to play with her cat. [non-finite clause]

Sub-ordinate clause:
A clause which is subordinate to some other part of the same sentence is a subordinate clause; for example, in 'The apple that I ate was sour', the clause *that I ate* is subordinate to *apple* (which it modifies).

Subordinate clauses contrast with co-ordinate clauses as in 'It was sour but looked very tasty.' (Contrast: main clause)

However, clauses that are directly quoted as direct speech are not subordinate clauses.

That's the building where Aldo lives. [relative clause; modifies building]
She watched him as he ate. [adverbial; modifies watched]
What you said was very unkind. [acts as subject of was]
She noticed an hour had passed. [acts as object of noticed]
Not subordinate: He shouted, "Look out!"

Relative clause:
A relative clause is a special type of subordinate clause that modifies a noun. It often does this by using a relative pronoun such as *who* or *that* to refer back to that noun, though the relative pronoun that is often omitted.

A relative clause may also be attached to a clause. In that case, the pronoun refers back to the whole clause, rather than referring back to a noun.

That's the girl who lives near school. [who refers back to girl]
The prize that I won was a book token. [that refers back to prize]
The prize I won was a book. [the pronoun that is omitted]
James broke the record, which impressed Samantha. [which refers back to the whole clause]

Co-ordinate clause:
Words or phrases are co-ordinated if they are linked as an equal pair by a co-ordinating conjunction, e.g. *and, but, or*. The difference between co-ordination and subordination is that, in subordination, the two linked elements are not equal.

Susan and Amy met in a café. [links the words Susan and Amy as an equal pair]
They talked and drank tea for an hour. [links two clauses as an equal pair]
Susan got a bus but Amy walked. [links two clauses as an equal pair]
Not co-ordination: They ate before they met. [before introduces a subordinate clause]

Cohesion
A text has cohesion if it is clear how the meanings of its parts fit together. Cohesive devices can help to do this. In the example, there are repeated references to the same

thing (shown by the different style pairings), and the logical relations, such as time and cause, between different parts are clear.

> A visit has been arranged for Year 6, to the Twin Peaks Field Study Centre, leaving school at 9.30am. This is an overnight visit. The centre has beautiful grounds and a nature trail. During the afternoon, the children will follow the trail.

Cohesive devices
Cohesive devices are words used to show how the different parts of a text fit together. In other words, they create cohesion.

> Julia's dad bought her a football. The football was expensive! [determiner; refers us back to a particular football]

Colons and semi-colons
Colon:
The colon is used to introduce a list. It serves to separate the main clause of the sentence from the list that follows. For example, 'There are a few essential items you will need to bring with you: a packed lunch, a drink and a waterproof coat.'
    Used in this way, a colon should not be used immediately after a verb or preposition. The above example would not work as 'You need to bring: a packed lunch ...'

Semi-colon:
The semi-colon is used to link two independent clauses that it would be grammatically accurate to write as two sentences. It is used when two ideas are considered to be close to use discrete sentences.

> Giles was angry; no-one would do as he asked.

These clauses describe a causal relationship between someone's feelings and the reason for those feelings, making the semi-colon appropriate. Another example, this time taken from Dickens, employs the semi-colon for a different reason.

> It was the best of times; it was the worst of times.

Here, the punctuation serves to emphasise how at a single point in time life was both happy and miserable. The punctuation serves to reinforce this.

Commas
Commas serve to sub-divide sentences in a few different ways. They are a common and useful punctuation mark and the rules around them are quite straightforward. Commas are not used to indicate a pause; this advice is unhelpful and will inhibit students' ability to genuinely understand their use.

- Commas separate the items on a list of three or more items. *Emma needed to buy toothpaste, shampoo and conditioner.* this example shows how the comma is used to separate all items in the list except the final two, which are linked by *and*. Another way of referring to this usage is that the comma works where *and* could be used.
- Commas serve to connect clauses in a compound sentence. *Amy thought that noodles and quiche would be a tasty lunch, and it turns out she was right.* The comma precedes a conjunction, and can be used in this way before *and, or, but, while* and *yet.*
- Commas isolate a subordinate clause within a complex sentence. In this usage they function in a similar way to brackets as they surround a relevant, though minor, piece of additional information. *Using commas well, I would argue, is an important skill for any writer.* In instances like this the commas isolate the subordinate clause which could be removed from the sentence without affecting the overall sense. <u>Using commas well is an important skill for any writer.</u>

Complement

A verb's subject complement adds more information about its subject, and its object complement does the same for its object. Unlike the verb's object, its complement may be an adjective. The verb be normally has a complement.

> She is our teacher. [adds more information about the subject, *she*]
> They seem very competent. [adds more information about the subject, *they*]
> Learning makes me happy. [adds more information about the object, *me*]

Compounding

A compound word contains at least two root words in its morphology; e.g. *whiteboard, superman.*

Compounding is very important in English. It is the most common way that we have for forming new words. A new idea or concept will often be defined by bringing two words together to form the new idea. A recent example would be 'credit crunch'. Other examples: blackbird, blow-dry, bookshop, ice cream, English teacher, inkjet, one-eyed, bone-dry, babysit, daydream, outgrow.

Conjunctions

You/we may have been used to the term 'connectives'. This has disappeared from the most recent strategy documents and is replaced by 'conjunctions'. A conjunction links two words or phrases together. There are two main types of conjunctions:

- co-ordinating conjunctions (e.g. *and*) link two words or phrases together as an equal pair:
- James bought a bat and ball. [links the words *bat* and *ball* as an equal pair]
- Kylie is young but she can kick the ball hard. [links two clauses as an equal pair]
- subordinating conjunctions (e.g. *when*) introduce a subordinate clause:

- Everyone watches when Kyle does back-flips. [introduces a subordinate clause]
- Joe can't practise kicking because he's injured. [introduces a subordinate clause]

Consonant

A sound which is produced when the speaker closes off or obstructs the flow of air through the vocal tract, usually using lips, tongue or teeth.

Most of the letters of the alphabet represent consonants. Only the letters a, e, i, o, u and y can represent vowel sounds.

> /p/ [flow of air stopped by the lips, then released]
> /t/ [flow of air stopped by the tongue touching the roof of the mouth, then released]
> /f/ [flow of air obstructed by the bottom lip touching the top teeth]
> /s/ [flow of air obstructed by the tip of the tongue touching the gum line]

Contraction

Contractions are shortened versions of two or more words. They are most commonly found in speech and informal writing. When used in the written form an apostrophe would be used to denote the absence of one or more letters. *I can't do it. I would've asked but I forgot. What's the time?*

The rule is that when contracting words in this way, the space between the words is removed and missing letters are replaced with an apostrophe. When children and young people learn that examples such as *could've* and *would've* are contracted versions of *could have* and *would have*, it can be a breakthrough moment in stopping the common mistake of writing *could of* or *would of*.

Determiners

A determiner specifies a noun as known or unknown, and it goes before any modifiers (e.g. adjectives or other nouns).

Some examples of determiners are:

- articles (*the, a* or *an*)
  the home team [article, specifies the team as known]
  a good team [article, specifies the team as unknown]
- demonstratives (e.g. *this, those*)
  that pupil [demonstrative, known]
- possessives (e.g. *my, your*)
  Julia's parents [possessive, known]
- quantifiers (e.g. *some, every*).
  some big boys [quantifier, unknown]

By way of contrast: *home the team, big some boys* [both incorrect, because the determiner should come before other modifiers].

Double negatives

There are a good number of acceptable double negatives. For example:

> It has not gone unnoticed.
> You can't not go.
> I am not unimpressed.

Ellipsis

Ellipsis is the omission of a word or phrase which is expected and predictable.

> Frankie waved to Ivana and she watched her drive away ... Frankie waved to Ivana and watched her drive away.
> She did it because she wanted to do it ... She did it because she wanted to.

Etymology

A word's etymology is its history: its origins in earlier forms of English or other languages, and how its form and meaning have changed. Many words in English have come from Greek, Latin or French.

> The word *school* was borrowed from a Greek word σχολή (skholé) meaning 'leisure'.
> The word *verb* comes from Latin *verbum*, meaning 'word'.
> The word *mutton* comes from French *mouton*, meaning 'sheep'.

Exclamation marks

An exclamation mark is a <u>punctuation</u> mark usually used after an <u>interjection</u> or <u>exclamation</u> to indicate strong feelings or high volume (shouting), and will often mark the end of a sentence, e.g. 'Look out!'

It can also used to add emphasis to a statement, e.g. 'C'mon the lads!'

Fronting

A word or phrase that normally comes after the verb may be moved before the verb: when this happens, we say it has been 'fronted'.

For example, a fronted adverbial is an adverbial which has been moved before the verb. When writing fronted phrases, we often follow them with a comma.

> Before we begin, make sure you've got a pencil. [Without fronting: Make sure you've got a pencil before we begin.]
> The day after tomorrow, I'm visiting my granddad. [Without fronting: I'm visiting my granddad the day after tomorrow.]

Full stops

Full stops are used to mark the end of a sentence. However, they also have a number of other uses. They are employed after initials (as in A. A. Milne and J. R. R. Tolkien).

Homonyms – homophone
Two different words are homonyms if they both look exactly the same when written, and sound exactly the same when pronounced.

> Has he left yet? Yes – he went through the door on the left.
> The noise a dog makes is called a bark. Trees have bark.

Two different words are homophones if they sound exactly the same when pronounced.

> hear, here
> some, sum

_I_ and _me_, the use of
You use _I_ when referring to the subject of a sentence or clause.
  You use _me_ when you are referring to the object of the sentence or clause.

Infinitives
A verb's infinitive is the basic form used as the headword in a dictionary (e.g. walk, be). Infinitives are often used:

* after 'to'; and
* after modal verbs.

> I want to cry. I will be honest.

Inflection
When we add _-ed_ to walk, or change mouse to mice, this change of morphology produces an inflection ('bending') of the basic word, which has special grammar (e.g. past tense _dogs_ is an inflection of _dog_, _went_ is an inflection of _go_ and _better_ is an inflection of _good_).

Modifiers
One word or phrase modifies another by making its meaning more specific. Because the two words make a phrase, the 'modifier' is normally close to the modified word.
  In the phrase 'secondary-school teacher':

* _teacher_ is modified by _secondary school_ (to mean a specific kind of teacher)
* _school_ is modified by _secondary_ (to mean a specific kind of school).

Nouns
Nouns can be thought of as 'naming words' because they name people, places and 'things'. Nouns may be classified as common (e.g. boy, day) or proper (e.g. Ivan,

Thursday), and also as countable (e.g. thing, boy) or non-countable (e.g. stuff, money).

- common, countable: a book, books, two chocolates, one day, fewer ideas
- common, non-countable: money, some chocolate, less imagination
- proper, countable: Marjorie, Ipswich, Wednesday

Object

An object is normally a noun, pronoun or noun phrase that comes straight after the verb, and shows what the verb is acting upon.

> Year 2 designed puppets. [noun acting as object]
> I like that. [pronoun acting as object]

Subject and object either side of a verb are the basic building blocks of a sentence. Often, when a student has written a fragment of a sentence it will be that the sentence has no subject. The missing subject is often in the previous sentence and the fragment that they have written would actually be better as a sub-clause of that previous sentence. For example:

> Simon looked at his computer excitedly. Packed with data that needed to be figured out.

Participles

Verbs in English have two participles, called 'present participle' (e.g. walking, taking) and 'past participle' (e.g. walked, taken). Unfortunately, these terms can be confusing to learners, because:

- they don't necessarily have anything to do with present or past time;
- although past participles are used as perfects (e.g. has eaten) they are also used as passives (e.g. was eaten).

> He is walking to school. [present participle in a progressive]
> He has taken the bus to school. [past participle in a perfect]
> The photo was taken in the rain. [past participle in a passive]

Passive (see Active)

Phrase

A phrase is a group of words that are grammatically connected so that they stay together, and that expand a single word, called the 'head'.

The phrase is a noun phrase if its head is a noun, a preposition phrase if its head is a preposition, and so on; but if the head is a verb, the phrase is called a clause. Phrases can be made up of other phrases.

> She waved to her mother. [a noun phrase, with the noun *mother* as its head]
> She waved to her mother. [a preposition phrase, with the preposition *to* as its head]
> She waved to her mother. [a clause, with the verb *waved* as its head]

Phrases – Noun phrase:
A noun phrase is a phrase with a noun as its head, e.g. 'some foxes', 'foxes with bushy tails'.

> Adult foxes can jump. [adult modifies foxes, so adult belongs to the noun phrase]
> Almost all healthy adult foxes in this area can jump. [all the other words help to modify foxes, so they all belong to the noun phrase]

Phrases – preposition:
A preposition phrase has a preposition as its head followed by a noun, pronoun or noun phrase.

> He was in bed.
> I met them after the party.

Plurals
The English language has a habit of having a grammatical rule and then several exceptions and patterns that stand outside the rule. Making plurals is a good example.

To make a noun plural you add an -s, e.g. apple – apples. However, there are six further patterns to follow.

Many nouns that end with a consonant and then a *y* change the *y* to *i* and add -es, e.g. baby – babies.

Nouns that end with a vowel and a *y* just add the -s, e.g. boy – boys.

Nouns that end in *ch* or *sh* or *ss* or *x* add an -es, e.g. church – churches, dish – dishes, glass – glasses, fox – foxes

Some nouns that end in *f* or *fe* change this to *v* and add the -es, e.g. half – halves, knife – knives.

Nouns ending with a vowel and then *o* add an -s, e.g. radio – radios.

Nouns ending with a consonant and then *o* add -es, e.g. tomato – tomatoes.

Just to make things extra difficult there are words for which the singular and plural forms are the same, e.g. sheep.

There are words that don't follow the patterns above, e.g. mouse – mice.

Possessives
A possessive can be:

• a noun followed by an apostrophe, with or without s;
• a possessive pronoun.

The relation expressed by a possessive goes well beyond ordinary ideas of 'possession'. A possessive may act as a determiner.

> Tariq's book [Tariq has the book]
> The boys' arrival [the boys arrive]
> His obituary [the obituary is about him]
> That essay is mine. [I wrote the essay]

Prefixes

A prefix is added at the beginning of a word in order to turn it into another word.

> overtake
> disappear

Prepositions

A preposition links a following noun, pronoun or noun phrase to some other word in the sentence. Prepositions often describe locations or directions, but can describe other things, such as relations of time. For example:

> Jasper waved goodbye to Martin. He'll be back from India in three months.

Words like *before* or *since* can act either as prepositions or as conjunctions.

> I haven't seen my dog since this morning.
> By way of contrast: I'm going, since no-one wants me here! [conjunction: links two clauses]

Progressive

The progressive (also known as the 'continuous') form of a verb generally describes events in progress. It is formed by combining the verb's present participle (e.g. singing) with a form of the verb be (e.g. he was singing). The progressive can also be combined with the perfect (e.g. he has been singing).

> Michael is singing in the store room. [present progressive]
> Amanda was making a patchwork quilt. [past progressive]
> Usha had been practising for an hour when I called. [past perfect progressive]

Pronouns

Pronouns are normally used like nouns, except that:

- they are grammatically more specialised;
- it is harder to modify them.

In these examples, each sentence is written twice: once with nouns, and once with pronouns.

Rachel waved to Martin.	She waved to him.
Nick's mother is over there.	His mother is over there.
The camping will be an overnight visit.	This will be an overnight visit.
Alan and Simon caused the problem.	They are the ones who caused the problem.

Pronouns can cause cohesion problems in the writing of your students. It needs to be clear to whom a pronoun refers. Often students get so involved with plot that they sometimes forget the construction of writing. Here is an example of the sort of problem that can occur when pronouns are not used clearly.

Greg and Miles saw Alan and Simon rushing towards them. All hope was lost. They had something important to tell them.

Who has something important to tell is not clear here? Difficult to know here.

Punctuation
Punctuation includes any conventional features of writing other than spelling and general layout: the standard punctuation marks . , ; : ? ! - – ( ) " " ' ' , and also word-spaces, capital letters, apostrophes, paragraph breaks and bullet points. One important role of punctuation is to indicate sentence boundaries.

Question mark
A question mark is used at the end of a direct question. It simply indicates that the sentence is a question. Informally, it is sometimes used in combination with other punctuation marks, although this is not considered to be correct in formal writing. For example, 'Why was he doing that?!'
    The main issue that you are likely to have in children's writing with the question mark is that it is missed out.

Received pronunciation
Received Pronunciation is regarded as the 'standard' accent of Standard English in the United Kingdom. RP is defined in the *Concise Oxford English Dictionary* as 'the standard accent of English as spoken in the south of England'. It can also be heard from native speakers throughout the United Kingdom. However, the vast majority of speakers are not RP speakers. Most have regional variations in how they speak, both in terms of regional vocabulary choices and regional accents.
    Whilst there is no linguistic reason for its superiority, RP enjoys a prestige in the United Kingdom. It has been seen as the accent of those with power, money, and influence. Since the 1960s, a greater permissiveness towards allowing regional English

varieties has taken hold in society. It is interesting for your students to consider the advantages and disadvantages of speaking with regional accents and dialects that move away from the 'norm' of RP.

Register
Courtroom proceedings, tennis commentaries and works of fiction use different registers of the same language, recognisable by the differences of vocabulary and grammar. Registers are 'varieties' of a language that are each tied to a range of uses, in contrast with dialects, which are tied to groups of users.

> I regret to inform you that Mr Joseph Smith has passed away. [formal letter]
> Have you heard that Joe has died? [casual speech]
> Joe falls down and dies, centre stage. [stage direction]

Schwa
The name of a vowel sound that is found only in unstressed positions in English. It is the most common vowel sound in English. It is written as /ə/ in the International Phonetic Alphabet. In the English writing system, it can be written in many different ways.

> /əlɒŋ/ [along]
> /bʌtə/ [butter]
> /dɒktə/ [doctor]

Semi-colons (see Colons)

Sentences, types of
A sentence is a group of words which are grammatically connected to each other but not to any words outside the sentence. The form of a sentence's main clause shows whether it is being used as a statement, a question, a command or an exclamation.

> You are my friend. [statement]
> Are you my friend? [question]
> Be my friend! [command]
> What a good friend you are! [exclamation]

A sentence may consist of a single clause or it may contain several clauses held together by subordination or co-ordination. Classifying sentences as 'simple', 'complex' or 'compound' can be confusing because a 'simple' sentence may be complicated, and a 'complex' one may be straightforward.

The terms 'single-clause sentence' and 'multi-clause sentence' may be more helpful.

> Ronnie went to his friend's house. He stayed there till tea-time.

Ronnie went to his friend's house, he stayed there till tea-time. [This is a 'comma splice', a common error in which a comma is used where either a full stop or a semi-colon is needed to indicate the lack of any grammatical connection between the two clauses.]

Ali went home on his bike to his goldfish and his current library book about pets. [single-clause sentence]

She went shopping but took back everything she had bought because she didn't like any of it. [multi-clause sentence]

Singular

Singular is one, for example *cat*, *dog* and *hat*. Plural is more than one, for example *cats*, *dogs* and *hats*.

Spelling, strategies

The Key Stage 2 strategy suggests a number of ways of approaching the active remembering of spellings. These include the following:

- sounding out phonemes to construct a word from its constituent sounds;
- to analyse words into syllables and other known words;
- to develop and then apply growing knowledge of spelling conventions and patterns;
- to use knowledge of common letter strings, visual patterns and analogies;
- to get your students to check their own spelling;
- to consider the spelling of words with inflectional endings.

Standard English and non-standard English usage

Standard English can be recognised by the use of a very small range of forms such as 'those houses', 'I did it' and 'I wasn't doing anything' (rather than their non-Standard equivalents); it is not limited to any particular accent. It is the variety of English which is used, with only minor variation, as a major world language. Some people use standard English all the time, in all situations from the most casual to the most formal, so it covers most registers. One of the aims of the national curriculum is that everyone should be able to use standard English as needed in writing and in relatively formal speaking.

I did it because they were not willing to undertake any more work on those houses. [formal standard English]

I did it cos they wouldn't do any more work on those houses. [casual standard English]

I done it cos they wouldn't do no more work on them houses. [casual non-standard English]

Stress
A syllable is stressed if it is pronounced more forcefully than the syllables next to it. The other syllables are unstressed.

Subject
The subject of a verb is normally the noun, noun phrase or pronoun that names the 'do-er' or 'be-er'. The subject's normal position is:

- just before the verb in a statement;
- just after the auxiliary verb, in a question.

Unlike the verb's object and complement, the subject can determine the form of the verb (e.g. 'I am', 'you are'). For example:

> Ronnie's <u>mother</u> went out.
> The <u>children</u> will study the animals.
> Will the <u>children</u> study the animals?

Suffixes
A suffix is an 'ending', used at the end of one word to turn it into another word. Unlike root words, suffixes cannot stand on their own as a complete word.

> teach – teacher [turns a verb into a noun]
> terror – terrorise [turns a noun into a verb]
> green – greenish [leaves word class unchanged]

Syllable
A syllable sounds like a beat in a word. Syllables consist of at least one vowel, and possibly one or more consonants.

> Cat has one syllable.
> Fairy has two syllables.
> Hippopotamus has five syllables.

Synonyms
Two words are synonyms if they have the same meaning, or similar meanings.

> talk – speak
> old – elderly

Tense
In English, tense is the choice between present and past verbs, which is special because it is signalled by inflections and normally indicates differences of time. In contrast,

languages like French, Spanish and Italian, have three or more distinct tense forms, including a future tense.

The simple tenses (present and past) may be combined in English with the perfect and progressive.

> He studies. [present tense – present time]
> He studied yesterday. [past tense – past time]
> He studies tomorrow, or else! [present tense – future time]
> He may study tomorrow. [present tense + infinitive – future time]
> He plans to study tomorrow. [present tense + infinitive – future time]
> If he studied tomorrow, he'd see the difference! [past tense – imagined future]

By way of contrast, here is an example of the three distinct tense forms in Spanish:

> Estudia. [present tense]
> Estudió. [past tense]
> Estudiará. [future tense]

Verbs

Verbs are sometimes called 'doing words' because many verbs name an action that someone has performed. This can be a way of recognising verbs, although it doesn't distinguish verbs from nouns (which can also name actions). Moreover many verbs name states or feelings rather than actions.

Verbs can be classified in various ways: for example, as auxiliary, or modal; as transitive or intransitive; and as states or events.

> He lives in Middlesbrough. [present tense]
> The teacher wrote a poem for the class. [past tense]
> He likes apples. [present tense; not an action]
> He knew my brother. [past tense; not an action]

Not verbs:

> The walk to Ivan's house will take an hour. [noun]
> All that adding up makes Simon so sleepy! [noun]

Verbs – auxiliary:
The auxiliary verbs are: *be, have, do* and the modal verbs. They can be used to make questions and negative statements. For example: 'Do you want an ice cream?' 'I don't want one, thanks.'

Verbs – finite:
Every sentence will typically have at least one verb which is either in the past or pres-

ent tense. These verbs are called 'finite'. The imperative verb in a command is also finite. Verbs that are not finite, such as participles or infinitives, cannot stand on their own: they are linked to another verb in the sentence.

Miles does the lunchtime shift every day. [present tense]
Even Greg did some teaching yesterday. [past tense]
Do the homework, Amy! [imperative]

Not finite verbs:

I have done them. [combined with the finite verb *have*]
I will do them. [combined with the finite verb *will*]
I want to do them! [combined with the finite verb *want*]

Verbs – intransitive:
A verb which does not need an object in a sentence to complete its meaning is described as intransitive. For example: 'We all <u>laughed</u>.' 'We would have liked to stay longer, but we had to <u>leave</u>.'

Your students might investigate the power of the intransitive verb. What impact does the use of the intransitive have? Does a sentence without that direct object create a different effect?

Verbs – modal:
Modal verbs are used to change the meaning of other verbs. They can express meanings such as certainty, ability, or obligation. The main modal verbs are *will, would, can, could, may, might, shall, should, must* and *ought*.

A modal verb only has finite forms and has no suffixes (e.g. *I sing – he sings*, but not *I must – he musts*). One really useful application of modal verbs that your students can be encouraged to explore is in creating tentativeness in their critical essay writing. Often students are very definite in their writing. For example, 'Dickens hates the upper classes.' You may want to modify the strength of this statement. So, 'Dickens may/might/must ...' These modals create a greater sense of a thoughtful writer/ reader, open to other perspectives and keen to debate.

Verbs – transitive:
A transitive verb takes at least one object in a sentence to complete its meaning, in contrast to an intransitive verb, which does not.

He loves Juliet.
She understands English grammar.

Vocabulary – active
A person's active vocabulary is that part of a language that they understand and of

which they are able to make use. A normal active vocabulary for a student in a high school would be somewhere between 12,000 and 17,000 words. There is an obvious benefit to having a large active vocabulary in finding ways to express yourself successfully.

There are a number of different active vocabularies that can be measured.

Reading vocabulary:
This is all the words that a literate person can recognise when they are reading. This is generally the largest type of vocabulary mainly because a reader tends to be exposed to more words by reading than by listening.

Listening vocabulary:
A person's listening vocabulary is all the words that they can recognise when listening to speech. It is entirely plausible that people may still understand words they have not been exposed to before by making use of cues such as tone, gestures, the topic of discussion and the context of the conversation.

Speaking vocabulary:
A person's speaking vocabulary is all the words that they use when speaking. It is likely to be a portion of the listening vocabulary. Due to the spontaneous nature of speech, words are often misused. This misuse – though slight and unintentional – may be compensated by facial expressions, tone of voice, or gestures.

Writing vocabulary:
Words are used in various forms of writing from formal essays to Twitter feeds. Many written words do not commonly appear in speech. Writers generally use a fairly limited set of words. As writers, we all tend to have favourite and routine ways of expressing ourselves.

Vocabulary – concision/precision
Concision:
Concision is the art of making sure that there are no unnecessary words or expressions in writing. Your students can be encouraged to think about concision as they draft their writing.

Precision:
Precision is the art of being exact as possible in writing. Your students can be encouraged to think about being precise as they reflect upon the writing that they have done. Do the words carry the sense of meaning that they had hoped to achieve? Are there words that could come out of the writing to be replaced with others that are closer to the desired effect?

Vowels
A vowel is a speech sound which is produced without any closure or obstruction of the vocal tract. Vowels can form syllables by themselves, or they may combine with consonants. In the English writing system, the letters a, e, i, o, u and y can represent vowels.

Word
A word is a unit of grammar: it can be selected and moved around relatively independently, but cannot easily be split. In punctuation, words are normally separated by word spaces. Sometimes, a sequence that appears grammatically to be two words is collapsed into a single written word, indicated with a hyphen or apostrophe (e.g. well-built, he's).

> headteacher or head teacher [can be written with or without a space]
> I'm going out.
> 9.30 am

Word class
Every word belongs to a word class which summarises the ways in which it can be used in grammar. The major word classes for English are noun, verb, adjective, adverb, preposition, determiner, pronoun, and conjunction.
   Word classes are sometimes called 'parts of speech'.

Word family
The words in a word family are normally related to each other by a combination of morphology, grammar and meaning.

> teach – teacher – teaching
> extend – extent – extensive
> grammar – grammatical – grammarian

Index

Terms in the glossary are in bold type.

accent 128–129
achievement: employment 57–58; sense of 45–46
active vocabulary: broadening 75–76; definition 133–134
adjectives 116
adverbs 116–117
analysis, cognitive level 13
antonyms 117
apostrophes: definition 117; exceptions to rules 80
application, cognitive level 12–13
art forms, grammer of 95–96
articles 117–118
attitudes to grammar 35–36
audiences: peer review 78; writing for 55–56
authors, contacting 105–106
autobiography 51–52

being silly 33–34
biography 51–52
blended words 42
brackets 118

choosing words to learn about 83
class discussions 76, 85–86
classes of words: playing with 100–102; skills 9
clauses 118–119
'Clever Signs' board 27
cognitive levels 12–13
cohesion 119–120
cohesive devices 120
colons 120
commas 120–121
Comment feature 24–25
common mistakes in spelling 84
complement of verbs 121
compounding 121
comprehension: cognitive level 12

computer based learning: cut and paste fun 91–92; researching words on the internet 83
concision 134
confusing words 72
conjunctions (connectives) 121–122
consonants 122
continuous (progressive) form of verb 127
contractions 122
'correct', being 35–36
cut and paste fun 91–92

descriptivist approach 35–36
determiners 122
dictionaries 41–42
difficult words and punctuation 89–90
discussions 76, 85–86
double negatives 123
drafting 77–79
dramatic readings 93–94

education without testing 14
ellipsis 123
Elvis/Elvez? 27–28
emoticons 67–69
employment, preparation for 57–58
essential knowledge 14–15
etymology 123
evaluation, cognitive level 13
exceptions to rules 80–81
exclamation marks 123
exploding sentences 47–48

failure, sense of 45–46
favourite words 37–38
feedback sheet 78–79
feelings about grammar 35–36
five word stretches, most frequent 73
flexing your vocabulary brain
foreign languages: as clue to redundancy 111; translating 98
formal written English 9–10

fronting 123
full stops 123
fun with grammar 33–34, 86, 91–92
functions of words 9

glossary of technical terms 1, 4
grammar: attitudes to 35–36; basic function
    of 3; and communication 1; current
    approach to teaching 3; in curriculum 1;
    fun with 33–34, 86, 91–92; innate ability
    97–99; of photography 95–96; proficiency
    in 8; redundancy in 110–111; of speech
    31–32
grammar t-shirts 70–71
grammar working wall 49–50
guessing next line of poem 98–99

handwriting 53–54
high-frequency language 73
homonyms/homophones: definition 124;
    distinguishing 72
Hughes, Ted 101

I, **use of** 124
infinitives 124
inflection 124
innate ability 97–99
internet, researching words on 83
invented language 110
irregularities and idiosyncracies in English
    65–66

Key Stage 2: knowledge requirements for
    teachers 9–11; support for teachers 8;
    testing 1, 2–3, 5
Key Stage 3: importance of 5; student-
    teacher relationships 5; support for
    teachers 6, 8; testing 2–3; transition to 7–8
knowledge: cognitive level 12; essential and
    specialist 14–15

language: exceptions 80–81; foreign *see*
    foreign languages; frequently used 73;
    innate ability 97–99; irregularities and
    idiosyncracies 65–66; meaning in 110;
    redundancy 109–111; sounds 110;
    systematic 110; translating other languages
    98
listening vocabulary 134

making up new words 87–88
marking tests 45
me, **use of** 124
memorising spelling 10–11, 83, 130
mistakes in spelling, dealing with 82, 84
modelling of process of writing 103–104

modifiers 124

narrative: biography and 51–52; building
    29–30
new punctuation marks and emoticons
new words, making up 87–88
non-standard English 9–10, 130
nouns 124–125

object of verb 125, 131
old words in dictionaries 41–42
openings to stories 103
'organic' spelling test 82

participles 125
PEE (Point/Evidence/Explanation) structure
    43–44
peer review 78
photography, grammar of 95–96
phrases 125–126
plurals: definition 126; exceptions to rules
    80–81
poetry: guessing next line 98–99; playing
    with word class 101
positive spelling test 83
possessives 126–127
precision 134
prefixes 127
prepositions 127
prescriptivist approach 35
Presley, Elvis 27–28
progressive (continuous) form of verb 127
pronouns 127–128
pronunciation, received (RP) 128–129
punctuation: definition 127–128; difficult
    89–90; exceptions to rules 80; new
    punctuation marks and emoticons 67–69;
    skills 10

question marks 128
questions 19–20, 85–86
quick word exercises 107–108

reading: dramatic readings 93–94; vocabulary
    134
received pronunciation (RP) 128–129
redrafting 77–79
redundancy: foreign languages as clue 111; in
    grammar 110–111; in language 109–111
registers (varieties) of language 129
ridiculous rewrites 75–76
'right', being 35–36

Sarcmark 67–68
scaffolding spellings 83–84
schwa 15, 129

self-commentary 24–25
semi-colons 120
sentences: exploding 47–48; ideas for
    teaching 21–23; length 43; PEE structure
    43–44; types of 129–130
signs: collecting 26–28; misspellings on 83
silly games 33–34, 86
singular 130
'sloppy language' 36
sorting out confusing words
sounds in English 110
speaking vocabulary 134
specialist knowledge 14–15
speech 31–32
spelling: common mistakes 84; confidence
    building 82; memorising 10–11, 83, 130;
    misspellings 82; mistakes, dealing with 82,
    84; 'organic' spelling test 82; positive
    spelling test 83; scaffolding 83–84; tips for
    82–84
standard English 9–10, 130
stories: biography 51–52; openings 103;
    telling 29–30, 59–60; Twitter 61–64
stress (on syllables) 131
student-teacher relationships 5
students: approaches to learning 1;
    aspirations 57; innate ability 97–99; self-
    commentary 24–25
subject of verb 125, 131
suffixes 131
support for teachers 6, 8
syllables: definition 131; stress on 131
synonyms 131
syntax 39–40
synthesis, cognitive level 13
systematic language 110

t-shirts 70–71
teachers: approaches to 'correctness' 35–36;
    knowledge requirements 3–4, 9–11;
    support for 6, 8
tenses 131
testing: achievement 45–46; cognitive levels
    12–13; culture of 2; education without 14;
    Key Stage 2 1; marking tests 45; 'organic'
    spelling test 82; positive spelling test 83;
    value given to 45–46; Year 6 SP&G test 3,
    9, 12

Thompson, Emma 36
tips for spelling 82–84
transition to Key Stage 3 7–8
translating other languages 98
Twitter stories 61–64

value given to tests 45–46
verbs: complement 121; definition 115–116,
    132–133; object and subject 125, 131;
    progressive (continuous) form 127
vocabulary *see* words
vowels: definition 135; *schwa* 15, 129
vulgar words 41

'Whoops!' board 26
Williams, William Carlos 98
word classes: playing with 100–102; skills 9
word endings 109
word families 135
word walls 76
Wordles 73–74
words: active vocabulary 75–76, 133–134;
    blended 42; broadening vocabulary 75–76;
    choosing words to learn about 83;
    concision 134; confusing 72; definition
    135; difficult words 89–90; etymology
    123; favourite 37–38; listening vocabulary
    134; making up new words 87–88;
    misspelt 82; most frequent five word
    stretches 73; old words in dictionaries
    41–42; plural 80–81; precision 134; quick
    exercises 107–108; reading vocabulary
    134; speaking vocabulary 134; vocabulary
    skills 10; vulgar 41; when is a word a
    word? 109; writing vocabulary 134
writing: ask the author 105–106; drafts
    77–79; feedback sheet 78–79; handwriting
    53–54; modelling of process of 103–104;
    peer review 78; for real audiences 55–56;
    ridiculous rewrites 75–76; standard
    English 9–10; value given to 31;
    vocabulary 134

Year 6: SATS 5; SP&G test 3, 9, 12;
    transition from 7
Year 7: starting 5; student-teacher
    relationships 5; support for teachers 6;
    teachers' work 5–6; transition to 7–8

Taylor & Francis eBooks

Helping you to choose the right eBooks for your Library

Add Routledge titles to your library's digital collection today. Taylor and Francis ebooks contains over 50,000 titles in the Humanities, Social Sciences, Behavioural Sciences, Built Environment and Law.

Choose from a range of subject packages or create your own!

Benefits for you

» Free MARC records
» COUNTER-compliant usage statistics
» Flexible purchase and pricing options
» All titles DRM-free.

Benefits for your user

» Off-site, anytime access via Athens or referring URL
» Print or copy pages or chapters
» Full content search
» Bookmark, highlight and annotate text
» Access to thousands of pages of quality research at the click of a button.

REQUEST YOUR **FREE** INSTITUTIONAL TRIAL TODAY	**Free Trials Available** We offer free trials to qualifying academic, corporate and government customers.

eCollections – Choose from over 30 subject eCollections, including:

Archaeology	Language Learning
Architecture	Law
Asian Studies	Literature
Business & Management	Media & Communication
Classical Studies	Middle East Studies
Construction	Music
Creative & Media Arts	Philosophy
Criminology & Criminal Justice	Planning
Economics	Politics
Education	Psychology & Mental Health
Energy	Religion
Engineering	Security
English Language & Linguistics	Social Work
Environment & Sustainability	Sociology
Geography	Sport
Health Studies	Theatre & Performance
History	Tourism, Hospitality & Events

For more information, pricing enquiries or to order a free trial, please contact your local sales team: www.tandfebooks.com/page/sales

 Routledge Taylor & Francis Group | The home of Routledge books

www.tandfebooks.com